Robert G. Middleton

Charting a Course for the Church

Snug Harbor or Open Sea

Judson Press ® Valley Forge

CHARTING A COURSE FOR THE CHURCH

Copyright © 1979
Judson Press, Valley Forge, PA 19481

Bible quotations in this volume are in accordance with the Revised Standard Version of the Bible, copyrighted 1946, 1952, 1971, 1973 © by the Division of Christian Education of the National Council of the Churches of Christ in the United States of America, and are used by permission.

Library of Congress Cataloging in Publication Data

Middleton, Robert G.
    Charting a course for the church.

    Includes bibliographical references.
    1. Christianity—20th century.   I. Title.
BR121.2.M47   261.8   79-9949
ISBN 0-8170-0844-6

The name JUDSON PRESS is registered as a trademark in the U.S. Patent Office.
Printed in the U.S.A.

TO MY SONS
Robert
Douglas
Jeffrey
David

Preface

As Christians face the decades of the eighties and beyond, it is clear that new directions are needed. The experiences of the fifties, sixties, and seventies have left us with no clear and cogent set of convictions to guide Christian witness in the social order. This is especially true of those who, in company with John C. Bennett, acknowledge the great significance in their lives of social gospel liberalism and Christian realism. These are the movements of thought and action which have been important factors in my attempt to live responsibly as a Christian. I have felt a need to assess where I am at the present time and how well equipped I am for the social struggle of coming decades. The pages of this book are my attempt to express my indebtedness to these two formulations of Christian social thought and to see what elements can be put together to serve in the future.

No great novelty is claimed. My conviction is that neither tradition can be rejected or accepted totally. An attempt must be made to look afresh at these two forms of Christian thought and determine the elements which have continuing validity. This is what is attempted in these pages.

I am grateful to friends and institutions for having provided incentive for me to work out these reflections. An invitation to deliver the Waterman Lecture in the First Baptist Church of Ann Arbor, Michigan, was an important stimulus. I thank O. Carroll Arnold for the invitation and for friendship over the years. I am grateful also to Dr. Leon Pacala, President of Colgate Rochester/Bexley Hall/Crozer Theological Seminary, for the honor of delivering the Rauschenbusch Lecture in 1976. It was a high point in my life, made very delightful by the gracious hospitality of Dr. and Mrs. Pacala.

There is no adequate way for me to express my gratitude to my wife Evelyn. Not only has she typed the manuscript, but also she has made helpful suggestions all through the process. My preacher-sons, Robert and Jeffrey, have discussed these themes with me and—no doubt to their great surprise—led me to modify some emphases. The dedication to them and to Douglas and David is a small acknowledgment of the great joy they have brought to my life.

—Robert G. Middleton

First Baptist Church
Birmingham, Michigan

Contents

Two Cheers for the Sixties[1]

No: not three cheers for the sixties. Since no historical period is wholly good, Christians have no warrant for unrestrained enthusiasm for any era. But surely it is proper to give two cheers for the sixties.

For some time we have been in the process of revising our assessment of the sixties, and more and more voices are being raised to tell us that the sixties constituted a period in which individual Christians and corporate Christian bodies abandoned their proper role and embraced social change as though it were the whole of faith. Because of this one-sided approach, we are now being told, in words but even more clearly in actions, that we need to repudiate the period, learn its lessons, and get back to the tasks resting upon Christians.

A careful distinction obviously needs to be made. Nobody would want to give even two cheers for a great deal of what went on in the sixties. What is cheered, in restrained but nevertheless real fashion, is the commitment to fundamental social change on the part of Christians. It is disturbing to notice how many who were part of that era, sharing in its actions and passions, now beat their breasts in public and confess such participation with a sense almost of shame. Needless to say, those who were opposed to the major thrusts of those years now experience the joy of loud "I told you so" choruses. Before the negative verdict is accepted without question, it is essential to inject a note which will make plain that the sixties were not a time of disgraceful aberration on the part of Christians personally and corporately, but a time when the basic intention was honorable and worthwhile—and, in the fullest sense of the word, faithful.

It is important to note what is being said. The refusal to give three cheers is deliberate because the period does not deserve such treatment; perhaps no period ever has, though some have been given such uncritical adulation. It must be admitted that there were many follies perpetrated in the sixties, but this hardly makes that time unique. Criticism of such follies is clearly needed, because it is the only source of correction of past ineptness and the only effective guard against present complacency. The inexorable scrutiny of the sixties has been helpful in revealing many of the inadequacies in both thought and action.

From the comfortable vantage point of hindsight, it is clear that we embraced inept strategies. In some instances we were simply carried along on a surging tide and never wanted to do any tough-minded evaluation of where it might be carrying us. The realization that the task of bringing about fundamental social change demands hard, disciplined thought as well as ardent passion was not grasped clearly in the sixties. It was assumed that good intentions, which were in plentiful supply, must assure good results. Purity of heart substituted for hardness of head, and lofty ideals were expected automatically to produce sound tactics.

No honest appraisal of the sixties can overlook these misguided programs. We are still close enough to the period to remember specific manifestations of inept strategies. The technique of confrontation, in which opposition was the major focus, was an inept strategy. Originating in a sense of the beautiful purity of one's own group, it led to a refusal to make any alliances with less pure groups. Young radicals, especially, showed this trait. The self-righteousness of the left led to a defensive self-righteousness of the middle and, of course, of the right. The result was that there were many small groups endlessly congratulating themselves on their purity but incapable of uniting in order to get anything significant accomplished.

Flirtation with violence was another inept strategy. Its results were similar to those in the case of confrontation. The opponent ceased to be someone to be persuaded; he was someone to be eliminated. Since society had proved so resistant to the techniques of peaceful change, the thing to do—the *only* alternative remaining—was to break the iniquitous system apart. Hence the swollen rhetoric: Smash the Establishment! Tear apart the structures! And, in the process, don't be hampered by old-fashioned scruples against violence. Let Franz Fanon, Che Guevara, Malcolm X, and others show you that violence is as American as apple pie and about the only way to change a society where the oppressors hold all the real power. We therefore saw a great deal of an outlook which, in the words of Robert Penn Warren in his Jefferson Lecture, "tends to degenerate into violence, often in the strange marriage of pathology and ideology so characteristic of our moment."[2]

This flirtation with violence had a strong strain of romanticism in it. Illustrated in this was a particularly glaring example of softheadedness. Ignoring the plain lesson of human experience, many operated on the assumption that violence would purify the cause which utilized it and the beauty of the end sought would compensate for the ugliness of the means employed. What was needed but lacking then was the clear insight of Alexander M. Bickel who put the matter in forthright terms:

> Another sort of limit on civil disobedience has to do with means. Violence must be a monopoly of the state. In private hands, whatever its possible misuses by the state, it is always an unjust weapon. . . . Yet the extended consequences could be foreseen in that our freedom is founded ultimately on respect for moral values and for law. Enough violent disorder, and men with helmets and guns will patrol the streets.[3]

The failure of elementary insight into the dynamics of social change produced most of the ineptness of the sixties.

Furthermore, the addiction to irrationalism was an inept strategy. Flight from reason was a pervasive mark of the sixties. It was produced, in part at least, by revulsion against the pathetic plight into which supposedly rational persons had led us. If reason gave us the technology which produced the ecological crisis; if reason, complete with computers and the latest in refined statistical expertise, landed us in the debacle of Vietnam; if a professedly rational society ended up confronting Watergate—if all this is the product of reason, then irrationalism becomes an understandable alternative. But what was not seen was that the flight into the irrational, whether the soft irrationalism of drugs or the strident, harsh irrationalism of sloganeering, was a poor substitute for the arduous discipline of trying to bring together lofty ideals and sound strategies.

Not only were many strategies inept but also our expectations were often extravagant. It was in the area of race relations that hopes soared far beyond possibilities. Certain events had such a thrilling quality to those who shared in them that the expectation was born that the fortress of prejudice, so long able to withstand attacks, must now be toppled. "We shall overcome" expressed not a distant goal but an immediate expectation. Forgetting the lessons which a couple of decades of realism in theology and social action should have taught, many cast aside the insight of Reinhold Niebuhr that society is simultaneously human fulfillment and frustration. Niebuhr himself and the movement of thought he launched were dismissed as too pessimistic. Nothing, it was believed, could stand in the way of the achievement of the high goals of The Movement.

What took place then should not have been unexpected. When it became clear that the struggles (race relations is only one illustration) were not going to be won easily or perhaps at all, there was a moment of crisis for those who had participated in the turmoil and difficulty. The dream which had inspired them was threatened, and they felt they could not abandon the dream without calling into question the validity of what they had attempted. This moment of crisis drove some to abandon nonviolence and to attempt to gain by force what they saw slipping steadily away. They would pound and shape events, by violence if necessary, in order to bring to reality the dream of a nonviolent society! For a period of time, the stridency and desperation of the tactics mounted as the goal grew more distant. One saw the strange phenomenon of young people who repudiated the "success" ethic but could find nothing else by which to dignify and justify their efforts.

The extravagant expectations and their inevitable disappointment produced in many a retreat from social involvement. For some it was a gentle withdrawal into the cozy world of private existence. For others it was a cynicism about human effort and an abandonment of any idealism. The reaction was produced because those who expected everything concluded that anything less than everything must equal nothing.

It must also be acknowledged that the period was one of theological superficiality. Its distinctive and best-known manifestation was the Death of God speculation, but this was only one of the indicators. The lure of the secular and the rather romantic visions of urbanism associated with it were another manifestation. The period moved erratically from one fad to another, lacking any clear focus or any sound principle of evaluation. There was, indeed, a brusque impatience with any emphasis on thought or reflection. The key word was action, and what did not result in action was unimportant. Out of this emphasis came the neglect of any concern about the disciplines of the religious life.

This recital does not exhaust the list by any means; it is only a sampling. Even this much, however, must raise a question: If all this was wrong, why give even two cheers for the sixties?

My answer is a stubborn insistence that the basic thrust of the churches in the sixties was right. For the first time on a significant scale the churches gave themselves with real seriousness to the task of bringing about fundamental social change in contemporary society. That effort, no matter what follies may have been associated with it, deserves some cheers; and it certainly deserves something better than the shabby treatment it is now getting in many quarters. When it is put over against the current complacency, it almost makes one want to rise up and give three cheers for that period.

It may be objected that the contention that the churches became interested in fundamental social change is misleading because such concern has always been part of the mission of the churches. Admittedly, the churches in America have had for many years agencies whose primary purpose has been to stimulate concern for social change and, in some instances, to formulate programs to bring about such change. It is no disparagement of such efforts, which have often been noble indeed, to point out that such social action agencies rarely shaped the policy of the church body. They were part of the structure, but almost never did they succeed in making their concerns the goals of the entire church body. Without undue cynicism, a strange case can be made for the contention that these groups functioned as a kind of "house conscience" for many denominations.

As long as they were raising their voices, circulating their petitions, and preparing their resolutions, the larger body could point to them as clear proof that social sensitivity did indeed dwell in American church circles. In a vicarious manner, the denomination lived on the social passion of its smaller bodies.

Something happened, however, in many church bodies in the sixties. The venerable, safe, supportive church establishment became concerned about achieving social change. Social action was no longer the effort of a little group which could be harmlessly indulged; the churches were putting their own lives on the line in behalf of oppressed and victimized people. The bureaucratic officialdom of the churches revolted against a society built upon structures of inhumanity and prejudice. It was the scope of this concern which was a new thing in American religion.

The result of such concern was predictable. Those who had been willing to tolerate social action bodies when they posed no threat to control of the entire church in its corporate dimension grew very uneasy. The alliance which had so long existed between the church and the status quo was threatened. For one of the few times in its American experience—perhaps for the only time—it seemed that the churches might become independent of the society around them. What H. Richard Niebuhr called "the captive church" was about to break out of captivity.

It was the threat posed by this possibility that frightened and upset many. The hold of the established order proved stronger than the imperative to change. To prevent the church from losing its place, many expressed their discontent by temporary withdrawal of presence and support. The institutional health, and perhaps even the survival, of the church was uncertain. Clearly, something had to be done; and we are now in the process of observing the attempt of the church to recover.

What is distressing is the disingenuous way in which the recovery is being sought. Few are willing to put the disenchantment with the sixties in terms of a repudiation of social concern and action. It could not be admitted that the attack on the churches was an attempt to divert these bodies from social agitation. Consequently, the reaction to the sixties is put in eminently high-sounding terms. The unconscious strategy has been to mount what is labeled a correction of the deficiencies of the sixties. But this strategy would not fool anyone. Under cover of the correction, what has really been attempted has been a change of direction. The sad fact is that the attempt has largely succeeded.

I have taken some pains to indicate my conviction that correction was needed, as it is always needed. But I have a strong suspicion that beyond legitimate criticism there is an attempt being made to turn the churches back to their accustomed role as supporters of the social system in which they are placed. Once again the church is to be taken safely captive. Even persons who have a genuine concern for social action, such as those who shaped the Hartford Appeal, betray this by a subtle lack of emphasis on their part in regard to social change. The informal group of theologians who drafted the Hartford Appeal were disturbed by what they regarded as the supine surrender of the churches to the forces of modern culture, and they stressed the need for the recovery of transcendence. While it was not the intention of the Hartford Appeal to deny social involvement, the silence of the Appeal on this issue is eloquent. John C. Bennett is surely right in calling attention to this neglect in the Hartford statement, pointing out that "their statement . . . seems to me to call for a retreat from much of the best that the churches have recently been doing to identify themselves with people around the world who are in greatest need of radical social change."[4] The point is that if this neglect could be manifested among persons like those who drafted the Hartford Appeal, it must be incredibly strong as a shaping force among others.

The evidence that the churches are settling back and ready to recover their past relationship of virtually unquestioning support is all about us. The concern for social change is weak and on the edges now. Almost through the seventies, I confess it is hard to muster even one cheer for this latter period.

When Martin Marty wrote his summary of the recent religious past and took a glance into the future in *The Fire We Can Light,* he came up with one of his typically perceptive images. He said that the religious forces in the sixties had been concerned about buffeting. The concern of the seventies, he felt, would be ballasting.[5] It is a suggestive figure of speech and nicely illumines the dilemma of religion today.

The religion of the sixties, for which I have been giving two cheers, clearly needed ballasting. The ship was on stormy seas, and it was not well equipped for the voyage. It got into some very rough seas and got tossed around a good bit because it had not provided for ballasting. But that ship was at least on the open sea, ready to face some storms, and it was headed, I contend, for the right port.

It would be unfortunate indeed if the religious ship of the seventies and eighties took very good care to arrange proper ballast—and then remained in a placid harbor, roped securely to the wharf. Ballast is intended, after all, to equip the ship for the open sea. The sixties deserve two cheers for being willing to be on open seas, struggling to reach a good harbor.

1

Our Present Plight

Strategy for Christian action in society must be worked out afresh in every generation. The fact that a given strategy was effective in past periods is not sufficient warrant for assuming that it will be just as effective in the present. As changes take place in the social order, a relevant Christian approach must be ready to alter some strategies in order to cope with new realities. Of course this is demanding and difficult, and the temptation is always strong to continue past policies simply out of inertia. Such an approach, however, is no longer adequate. A basic assumption behind these pages is that we need to absorb the lessons of the sixties, alter the directions taken in the seventies, and thus prepare for more effective action in the eighties.

Reviewing the Past

There is fondness in Christian circles for describing our venture in terms of a pilgrimage. The word conjures up a picture of a people following in the footsteps of Abraham, willing to leave settled abodes and go out seeking another land. It is questionable, however, if the word accurately describes Christians. For there is a disturbing human tendency to stay put, to insist that we are in the right place and that there is no good reason for moving from where we are. All along the way we have tended to transform resting-places into destinations.

It is therefore very difficult for us to see that we are always in need of evaluating critically our ways of proceeding. No Christian strategy can ever be more than an interim tactic. The one thing which remains constant is the calling of the Christian to bear witness to the lordship of Jesus Christ in the social order. The strategies in terms of which that calling is to be carried out are always relative and instrumental. No strategy, however noble and even holy it may seem, is eternal. It is meant only for the period "between the times," and to realize this is to be prepared to treat strategies from the past with gratitude for their effectiveness and with freedom that permits them to be altered in the light of new conditions and demands.

This task would be made easier, perhaps, if past strategies could be completely abandoned and entirely new ones brought into being. But this is rarely if ever possible. The task is made complex because we have to preserve certain features of the past and introduce those new elements which will permit us to develop a strategy adequate for our day. The new elements, however, always confront resistance, because the old is invested with a high value.

The attraction of the old is based in part upon an emotional commitment. The strategies were hammered out quite often in difficult circumstances; the cost of doing this was high in terms of anguish. Also involved in this is the fact that many of the strategies came to participants bearing names that were venerated. Given these two factors—the development of the strategy under the pressure of costly witness and the association of the strategy with highly respected names—it was hard to see that such strategies were instrumental. Useful in a particular time, they needed to be revised in most instances and rejected outright in others. To see this is always a dismaying task, because the struggles to develop and implement the strategies were virtually made identical with the Christian witness itself. To abandon such strategies, then, came to seem an act of betrayal.

Our present plight is created in part at least because we have arrived at our situation with a considerable amount of equipment from the past. It is necessary to see this clearly if we are to deal constructively with the contemporary need. It would be, of course, a gross oversimplification to contend that Christian strategies arrange themselves neatly into decades. Existence is simply not that accommodating! To assign a dominant character to any decade involves some distortion; but if this is recognized and allowance made for it, the practice is helpful.

The forties found Christians concerned, along with all others, about global conflict. During and following the hostilities, the churches sought the establishment of a "just and durable peace," hoping thereby to justify in some measure the sacrifices made in the war. The fifties found the Christian churches, in concert with the rest of the nation, anxious to pick up the threads of life again. It was a time of conventional piety and ecclesiastical prosperity. The religious "boom" persuaded many that everything must be well in Zion; the president commended faith, no matter in what; churches were crowded; new buildings were going up; the suburbs were scenes of churches humming with activities and filled with people. The sixties burst upon a people quite unprepared for what was to take place. Neither the forties nor the fifties gave indications to most people that things were fundamentally wrong and that Christians, of all persons, should be actively engaged in correcting such conditions. Hence the sixties exploded—demonstrations, marches, picketing for human rights and against war. The introverted piety of the fifties was turned outward by sheer force, until the impression was conveyed that to be on the sidelines was not only an evidence of timidity; it was almost an act of apostasy.

For a time the apostles of action carried the day against those who felt it inappropriate—to use no stronger word—for the churches to be so involved. But gradually the churches, as we have seen, found that the results were not as wondrous as partisans had hoped. They also found that sources of support, both personal and financial, began to disappear. The message was being communicated in unmistakable terms. A reaction set in; and, in terms of the figure of speech in the Prologue, the ecclesiastical ship changed course, sought a snug harbor, determined to make an inventory of its cargo and to give careful thought to the determination of its future course. The ship is now where we left her at the end of the Prologue—firmly tied to the wharf.

The present plight of the churches will, of course, be greeted with varying reactions. Some will rejoice in the return to port, sure that this is where the ecclesiastical ship ought to be. Others will lament such a situation, just as sure that the ship should be on the open seas. For the moment, I'd like simply to accept Martin Marty's depiction of the situation. This is, indeed, where we are. What is important is to try to understand what has brought us to this plight and what needs to be done in the present situation. It is a venture in terms of strategy for the churches which needs the mood and spirit of Lincoln's words as applied to the political sphere: "If we could first know where we are and whither we are tending, we could better judge what to do and how to do it."

Why a Cessation of Activity?

The sedate seventies should not have come as a complete surprise. A reaction of some sort was inevitable after the strenuous sixties. No favorable principle exempts Christian bodies from being governed by the same forces which influence and control other areas of existence. Following the exertions and tensions of the sixties, a period was needed in which to assess what had been accomplished, what had not been done, and what needed to be done in the new setting. This was one of those fundamental needs to which Arthur M. Schlesinger, Sr., drew attention some years ago in a celebrated essay in *The Yale Review*. He dealt with changing tides in American politics and pointed out how a period of vigorous reform was followed by one of calm and conservative reaction.

To apply the Schlesinger thesis to American social Christianity does not mean that there is some iron law which controls us. Its application does suggest, however, that the thesis illumines many areas of human affairs and that what we are now experiencing, in both our political and our religious realms, should not come as a complete surprise. The recognition of the reality of tides in politics and religion cautions against undue consternation when discouraging tendencies become visible.

Another possibility should also be mentioned. This same recognition can moderate our tendency to imagine that some monstrous betrayal has taken place. Because the issues are so important, there is always the danger of acting as though all who differ are worse than mistaken; they are, almost by definition, looked upon as deficient in dedication. What the Schlesinger thesis suggests is that the human spirit can be stretched taut for only a limited period of time; then there is need for some relaxation of the tension. I recognize, of course, that the crucial question is *how long* that period of relaxed tension should last. The greater our capacity to avoid self-righteous denunciations of each other, surely the greater will be our ability to arrive at a policy which will be both constructive and faithful.

Many persons within the churches of America will certainly rejoice that the ardent witness of the sixties is over. They may look at that battered ship at the wharf, its deck somewhat dirty, its masts broken, its crew minimal, and feel that they have been abundantly justified in their judgment that the ship was never intended to be on open seas. It was meant for nothing more than smooth sails around a sheltered cove. That is what it was built for, and really that's about all it could ever be expected to do.

It hardly needs to be emphasized at this late date that this is a viewpoint characteristic of a sizable segment of Protestant opinion. Any suggestion that Christian existence demands a witness in the public arena is strenuously opposed by this numerous group. By no means does the group condemn all social action; it tends to be selective, approving certain causes and avoiding others. It is often the case that members of this group see nothing whatever questionable about legislating personal morality, as in prohibition or in attacks on pornography. But any hint that churches should be concerned about political matters, which means anything other than personal morals, is indignantly rejected. This is certainly a familiar story by now; yet it is often overlooked by many commentators. There is a tendency to confuse the statements originating from certain academic areas or from denominational headquarters with the opinions of church members themselves. Fortunately or unfortunately, depending upon one's point of view, such statements fall far short of accurately expressing the feelings of the great bulk of American Christians. Those who have been described as Private Protestants, which means people who believe that religion has to do with matters of personal existence, are a large group in American church circles. I see little evidence that Public Protestants are likely to take over the churches in the near future.

Any attempt to understand where we are in social Christianity in modern America has to come to grips with the fact sketched here. The bulk of American Protestants either flatly reject any call to social witness or practice it with timidity and reluctance, usually within a certain narrow sector. It is not, therefore, accurate to say that social Christianity has been tried and rejected. Except for a minority within church circles, it has never been attempted on a continuing basis.

If the sixties had produced a shining list of triumphs, the ranks of Private Protestants might have seen defections. Success, especially in America, is the validation of all things, and this would have been the case in this area as well. But a shining list of victories is precisely what eluded us in the sixties. While a case can be made for the reality of some gains in that strife-filled period, there is no way that we can substantiate the assertion that all the aims of the period were realized. Indeed, it was the loftiness of the goals which turned out to be a serious disadvantage. The Private Protestants focused attention, not so much on what was achieved, but rather upon the extravagantly high goals set forth by those involved in the social struggle. The Private Protestants then used the goals stated by the Public Protestants as an instrument with which to attack social Christianity. It remains a strange irony that the social witness of the sixties should have been vulnerable to attack on the basis of its own unrealistic goals. Hence the aura of "success" never really touched the labors of the sixties.

In this situation, which saw withdrawals from the churches of many people and the shrinking of funds as a result, it was not surprising that bureaucracies became apprehensive. Since it is a fundamental assumption underlying these pages that religion can't live apart from some institutional embodiment, it is not possible to be nonchalantly indifferent to the fate of church bodies. A measure of sympathy for the bureaucrats—a term I use with no pejorative intent—is indicated. For they confronted the dismaying picture of streams of people leaving the churches and saw this taking place at both ends of the spectrum. What was left on their hands were gravely weakened church bodies.

From the left the churches were losing those who felt that not even the ardors of the sixties were sufficient. The churches, these persons concluded, could never become effective instruments of fundamental social change. They therefore made their exit, some with genuine sadness, some with embittered disappointment.

At the same time a procession was going out the other side of the spectrum. These were people who believed that what the churches had embarked upon in the sixties was, quite simply, a distortion of their real purpose. They had forsaken a ministry to the souls of persons for the sake of chasing some will-o'-the-wisp of social righteousness. In the course of this ill-conceived venture, they had involved the churches in enterprises which necessitated debilitating compromises and left the religious bodies unable to carry on a genuinely spiritual ministry. Such people became convinced that the only way to recover the churches was to withdraw support and presence and then, when such tactics had grievously weakened the churches, step back in and claim anew their control.

Church bureaucrats were in the unenviable position of being caught in the pressures of these two groups. It was not an easy spot, and human wisdom is hard put to find any way by which both groups could be satisfied. Perhaps to gain time, and in the process to let feelings cool down a bit, the leaders decided they had to seek haven for a while and then determine the next direction. Given the responsibilities they bore, such a decision is neither surprising nor culpable.

In light of this analysis, it is clear that two forces united to moderate the churches' commitment to social change. One was the consistent pressure of those who were convinced that such action had never been a proper expression of the basic purpose of the churches. The other was from those who were responsible for the institutional vitality and perhaps survival of the churches. They had been forced to recognize that vitality would be lost and survival was questionable if the social ardor continued unabated. The seventies have been a period when the churches have been trying to find a way by which to deal with these opposing pressures.

It would be unrealistic, however, to ignore another element which played a role in bringing about this lull in social action. There is an undeniable element of weariness which sets in. Social struggles, when they are participated in over a long period of time, take a significant toll on human energy and resources. The "tired" liberal is a stock figure, but this should not hide the fact that the tiredness is real. For a time the loftiness of the goals, the thrill of being involved in a cause which is manifestly right and just, the contagious power of shared concern with others, the spirit generated in the face of intransigent opposition—all of this is, for a time, capable of sustaining effort and inspiring dedication. But this can't be done indefinitely. The time comes when the spirit is no more willing than the flesh. While the essential rightness of the cause is not questioned, the energy needed to sustain effort is just not available.

It may well be the case that such weariness afflicts any social cause, but it is especially likely when the cause engenders hopes that are impossibly high. As soon as it becomes clear that the hopes, no matter how nobly conceived, can never be achieved, weariness can take over. The temptation at that point is either apathy or cynicism. The social action of the sixties, especially in the field of civil rights, left many "walking wounded" in its train.

Robert Coles provides an illustration of this in one of his essays dealing with his observation of the students who went to the South during the civil rights struggle. He was impressed with the remarkable commitment these young people demonstrated to their cause. The Movement galvanized their energies, and in the course of their involvement they endured enmity, beatings, murder, and jail. Their action was an impressive testimony to the power of idealism in our day. After sharing in their life, Dr. Coles saw the reality of weariness:

> But my own observations and those of many leaders in the civil rights groups lead me to say that weariness touches almost all the students who stay in the Movement for any significant period of time—that is, long enough to taste its hard, grinding daily demands which are not always relieved by spectacular successes and are often encumbered with the additional burden of hopes sparked but not realized.[1]

He goes on to point out that no one particular type of student is more likely to succumb to this weariness than another; it touches different types of human beings equally. When this weariness hits, it is necessary to find some respite, by moving away from the immediate tension, perhaps later to return.

I do not mean to suggest that people in the churches generally were involved in social change in anything approaching the degree of the students. But there were many in the churches whose emotional and spiritual energy was invested in the admirable hope that a new and better social order might emerge out of the labors and hardships of the sixties. They did not have to go South themselves in order to follow with keen interest what was happening there. Furthermore, there were many in the churches who shared in the struggles in their own communities, feeling a bond with many others who similarly invested themselves in good causes. Animated by a passion for justice born of serious concern with Christian beliefs, they wanted to see justice established and dignity defended for those who had so long known oppression. A victory in a lunch-counter desegregation struggle for a group of students was, in some real way, their victory as well. And, similarly, a defeat, a setback, a realization of how solidly entrenched were the forces of oppression became for them a crisis of morale. The phrases used by Dr. Coles to apply to the students in the South could also be applied to many in the churches—"hard grinding daily demands . . . not always relieved by spectacular successes" and the problem of coping with the "burden of hopes sparked but not realized." Such phrases catch the mood of many in the aftermath of the sixties. The students had to go home, away from the immediate context of the struggle. Perhaps that same need is partly responsible for the yearning for a haven on the part of many Christians. Time was needed for recovery and reevaluation, and this may well be a part of the meaning of the seventies.

Responsible social witness is an indispensable part of authentic Christian existence. When that is said, however, there is an immediate danger. The assertion tends to polarize the Christian community, ranging on one side those who affirm the assertion and on the other side those who deny it. Having thus divided, the respective sides often tend more to hurl indictments at each other than to explore the meaning of Christian living in this era. The air is filled with the dust of controversy, and often enough the real issues are lost. The matter is reduced to simplistic terms by each side. The "others" are not mistaken, perhaps even misguided; they are apostate. In such an atmosphere there is little that can be done to enlighten one another. Surely, one of the tasks of the Christian community now is to create an atmosphere of love and concern which will enable us to share with each other, sustained by the hope that out of such sharing there may come a clearer understanding of what the churches ought to be doing.

Such an atmosphere may be created if we can see what it is that has brought us to our present position. What we have to deal with is the honest opinion of many that Christians have no business being involved in social action. They want the ship to stay in port and certainly never to venture beyond the cove. Others want the ship overhauled, its damages repaired, a crew secured—but then it is to leave the port and head for open seas. This difference of viewpoints is a continuing and important issue, and it will be settled better in an atmosphere of mutual respect and affection than in one of discord and animosity.

Rauschenbusch and Niebuhr

An additional reason for the situation of the ecclesiastical ship should be mentioned. The crew of the ship, charged with sailing the seas of social relevance, fell into some serious differences of opinion. It was nothing like a mutiny, but it was nevertheless sharp and real disagreement. It could be overlooked completely when the sun was shining and real progress was being made toward some desired destination. The disagreement became a matter of consequence only when seas became rough and changes in direction and destination had to be made.

Now that the ship is in port there is a chance to assess this disagreement, trace its outlines, identify the protagonists, and try to determine whether there is a way by which the two groups can work through their differences. The groups in mind are those which have taken with real seriousness the claim of social involvement. One strain will be called the Rauschenbusch strain, gathering up those who have been shaped in outlook by the social gospel movement stemming from Gladden, Rauschenbusch, and others. The other strain will be called the Niebuhr strain, gathering up those who have been influenced by the movement of Christian realism.

The Rauschenbusch strain represents a noble vision of a society transformed by the power of Christian action. The degree of transformation expected by Rauschenbusch himself and those who followed him is still a matter of debate, but there is no question that he and those in the social gospel tradition were confident that society could be Christianized to a significant degree. Rauschenbusch believed that such a task was not only possible, but he believed that it was also well under way toward completion during his own lifetime.

The Niebuhr strain, on the other hand, injected into Christian social action a somber awareness that, no matter how high our aspirations may be, regardless of how laudable, even holy, our motivations, the actual results achieved will always be less than our hopes lead us to expect and far more compromised than our easy consciences permit us to acknowledge. This realism was forged in direct contrast to the surging optimism of the social gospel.

The two strains have always been in tension. This tension has not only been felt between groups, but it has also been internalized as a continuing perplexity within many participants in social Christianity. Moreover, it is not a tension which has antiquarian interest only; there are a great many persons today in whom the strains of the Rauschenbusch and the Niebuhr traditions remain in real conflict.

A personal word may be appropriate at this point, not because my own pilgrimage is important to anyone else, but because it may be illustrative of a similar spiritual journey taken by others. Educated in the early forties, my orientation to religion was decisively shaped by the Rauschenbusch tradition. He had been my father's teacher, and I received from my father Rauschenbusch's three major books. The impact made upon me in reading those books during high school days is something I can still remember. As a result, I was nurtured on the high hopes of that tradition. Pacifism in the Fellowship of Reconciliation and socialism in the Fellowship of Socialist Christians became the vehicles for my idealistic zeal. The kingdom of God, a central concern of Walter Rauschenbusch, was not looked upon as a consummation at the end of the age to be achieved only in some otherworldly realm. It was meant for this earth. Rauschenbusch said:

> It is a conception for this life here of ours, because Jesus says, "Thy kingdom come. Thy will be done" here. It is something that is here on this earth; that quietly prevades all humanity; that is always working toward the perfect life of God. . . . The perfect community of men—that would be the Kingdom of God![2]

The marks of this perfect community of men were indicated by Rauschenbusch in *A Theology for the Social Gospel* when he said the kingdom

> implies a progressive reign of love in human affairs. We can see its advance wherever the free will of love supersedes the use of force and legal coercion

as a regulative of the social order. This involves the redemption of society from political autocracies and economic oligarchies; the substitution of redemptive for vindictive penology; the abolition of constraint through hunger as part of the industrial system; and the abolition of war as the supreme expression of hate and the completest cessation of freedom.[3]

That was a noble vision and probably expressive of an idealism which should be embraced by a person at an appropriate stage of his or her development. It may have been naive; it was not ignoble.

It was not, however, an outlook which equipped one to deal with a world in severe crisis. And the world was in desperate crisis. A devastating economic depression created suffering on a wide scale and that problem held on until the coming of World War II. Then it was necessary somehow to absorb a world in which Buchenwald and Auschwitz were realities. Not long after our enemy's concentration camps were revealed, we became the instruments of the frightful havoc of Hiroshima and Nagasaki. Any idea that we inhabited a cozy world was shattered. A severe blow was dealt to our self-esteem, and we were not quite so complacently secure in our estimate of our own virtue. Innocence could not survive intact through such experiences. Accordingly, it was necessary to revise our outlook and in many instances to try to put back together a spiritual landscape which had been torn apart. The writings of Reinhold Niebuhr helped many to do just that. He provided a framework which enabled many to understand the world we lived in and to continue in the name of Christian faith to struggle to change conditions.

To go from the idealism of Rauschenbusch to the realism of Niebuhr was hardly a comfortable journey. The adjustment of outlook required by the impact of events was not an easy experience to endure. A great gulf separates Rauschenbusch's confidence from Niebuhr's somber realism. Two statements will illustrate this. In 1907 Walter Rauschenbusch wrote a letter to the Marlboro Conference of the Brotherhood of the Kingdom in which he said he was "impressed with the amazing changes in public thought since the Brotherhood was founded" and that all the things for which they stood—better politics, "the abolition of privilege, the rights of the people against the corporations"—were more and more becoming realities in American life.[4] Some twenty-five years later, chastened by World War I, the falsity of the twenties, the seriousness of the depression, totalitarian fury, and World War II, Reinhold Niebuhr stated that it is "safe to hazard the prophecy that the dream of perpetual peace and brotherhood for human society is one which will never be fully realised. It is a dream prompted by the conscience and insight of individual man, but incapable of fulfillment by collective man."[5] Those statements summarize rather well the difference in outlook between the Rauschenbusch tradition and the Niebuhrian challenge.

This is not simply an antiquarian issue. What strikes one who knew the forties and then lived through the sixties is the similarity in the optimism of the two periods. The forties, with the war over and the peace to be established, had high hopes. Something happened to those hopes, which Niebuhr's thought should have prepared us to expect; but evidently the American experience has a peculiar ability to generate tremendously high expectations. Such lofty goals may be set aside for a time, as realism moderates confidence; but they are rarely permanently abandoned. Whatever else may be said of it, the decade of the sixties saw a resurgence of extravagantly hopeful expectations. It was believed that a new day was truly coming and was almost here, and that only a bit more effort was required to bring it fully into being.

The central symbol of that confidence was the March on Washington. Godfrey Hodgson writes:

> The March on Washington was perhaps the last moment when that confidence was still possible. The magical moment when Mahalia Jackson's high note on the word "free" in the last line of the national anthem still hung in the air over the dusty crowd has been remembered by those who were there as the last glimpse of sunlit prospects glimpsed across stormy waters. The March on Washington did not represent the opening of a new period, but the end of the time of marching and praying.[6]

On that occasion the invocation was offered by Benjamin Mays. A bit later Mr. Hodgson interviewed Dr. Mays. "'After the March on Washington,' he told me thoughtfully, 'and after Martin's speech, and the entire nation praising it as a great event, it was inevitable that black people should feel that this is the moment, and this is the time, and the things we've been struggling for, for centuries, are just about at hand now.

"'Well,' said Dr. Mays, 'it's never so.'"[7] Mahalia Jackson's soaring "free" symbolizes the lofty idealism of the Rauschenbusch tradition.

The somber "it's never so" of Dr. Benjamin Mays symbolizes the Niebuhr strain. Much depends upon whether the two strains can be so harmonized that there can be what George H. Sabine calls, in a fine phrase, "an idealism without illusions and a realism without cynicism."[8]

This need calls for a careful assessment of the spirit of our era. There are times when idealism is needed to bring fresh vigor and vitality to a tired and disenchanted age. There are also those periods when pretensions and extravagant expectations need to be punctured by the astringent outlook of the realist. The present moment is one in which the soaring expectations of the sixties have been totally abandoned. The danger we now confront is found, therefore, at other points.

One danger is that the social imperative will be abandoned and Christian faith once again will be rigorously restricted to the private sphere. This individualistic proclivity has always been strong in American religion, and it would be foolish to imagine that its appeal is over.

A second danger is that of apathy produced when great efforts yield meager results. There has been plenty of such defeat, and the weariness, like of that of the students mentioned by Robert Coles, takes its toll. Apathy is the understandable response of those who say, "We tried so hard, oh, so hard! And see how things have stayed the same. We can't do anything more."

A third possible response is that of those who end up embittered and cynical. The sadness of apathy is canceled out and gives way to the bitterness of cynicism. Cynics feel something more than disappointment; they feel personally betrayed. They do not adjust their goals; they spurn any idealism.

If this analysis is reasonably accurate, it is clear that social Christianity is at a point of reassessment. This is nothing new and is no cause for alarm. The movement of social Christianity has already passed through various phases and will do so again; this is what is meant by treating all strategies as interim tactics. The early phase was the *pioneering* phase, when great figures like Washington Gladden and Walter Rauschenbusch rescued from neglect a form of Christian witness which had long been dormant. The second phase was that of *consolidation*, when the insights of the pioneers found embodiment in the curricula of theological seminaries and in the operations of church bodies. This was followed by the phase of *confidence*, when it seemed for a moment that the high goals of social Christianity might indeed be established in the social order. From such a period events precipitated us into a *disenchantment* phase. This is where many now find themselves, and hence there is need for transition into the next phase which is that of *reconstruction*.

A Needed Reconstruction

This reconstruction phase will involve struggles on several fronts. A continuing attempt must be made to demonstrate the inescapable social imperative in Christian faith. In addition, there will certainly be need for the development of theological depth which will enable the protagonists of social Christianity to live in a time of partial victories and of discouraging defeats. In some fashion, the continuing tensions between the Rauschenbusch and the Niebuhr strains will have to be resolved. Clearly, this is a formidable agenda and there are no guarantees of success. The thesis of this book, however, is that the attempt must be made. What remains is to outline some of the new emphases which need to be incorporated into social Christianity in order to fit it for the responsibilities now confronted.

If the ship is to put out from harbor and sail the stormy seas of the eighties, what changes need to be made in outlook and strategy? These changes will occupy us in the following chapters.

2

The Need for Independence

Christians have always been in tension about the proper relation between the churches and the society. The uncertainty has left the churches poised in indecision, uncertain whether to flee from society in revulsion or to fawn over it in adulation. Christians have tried to resolve the dilemma in one of two ways. Often religious bodies have fled from society in pursuit of an imagined purity. Just as often they have operated in servile dependence. Rarely encountered is a posture on the part of the churches which achieves independence while avoiding irresponsibility.

Sometimes a fundamental orientation is determined because, at a particularly impressionable moment, a certain book spoke directly and powerfully to one. Such a book for me was *The Church Against the World.* I can remember back in the 1940s purchasing it for 20 cents in a second-hand bookstore in Philadelphia. It was a real bargain for me! It was not a big book, either in size or in intention; but it was, I thought, profound in its analysis and cogent in its argument. It stated a basic approach to the role of the churches in American society, and the thesis of the book has remained important to me through the years.

The book was written by three men, then young, two of them

theological professors and the other a layman and politician. Intended, as the authors suggested, as a tract for the times, a manifesto, written to a threatened church from within the church, it retains its pungency in the 1970s and indicates that the call has lost none of its importance in the intervening years. The call then was for the church to break out of its captivity, to recover an authentic sense of its independence, and hence to fulfill the mandate received from its Head. That call, I am convinced, needs to be set forth as part of the agenda now before the churches.

The Church and the World

That little book set the tone for my conviction of what Christian mission is all about. H. Richard Niebuhr, Wilhem Pauck, and Francis P. Miller, the authors, spoke so persuasively, I am sure, because they were persons committed to the Christian community. "The point of view," H. Richard Niebuhr wrote, "is from within the church, is that of churchmen who, having been born into the Christian community, having been nurtured in it and having been convinced of the truth of its gospel, know no life apart from it."[1] While admitting that the church must of course pay attention to critics from without, the essay argued that much of the criticism was an attempt to turn the church away from its own standards and to shape its mission in conformity to other sources. Some of these persons, Niebuhr said,

> appear to direct their questions to it rather than to raise them as members of the community. They seem to criticize the church by reference to some standard which is not the church's but that of civilization or of the world. Apparently they require the church to engage in a program of salvation which is not of a piece with the church's gospel. They demand that it become a savior, while the church has always known that it is not a savior but the company of those who have found a savior.[2]

Thus the essential question for the church "is not how it can measure up to the expectations of society nor what it must do to become a savior of civilization, but rather how it can be true to itself: that is, its Head."[3] The basic crisis, then, "is not the crisis of the church in the world, but of the world in the church."[4]

Back of the thesis of this tract for the times was obviously a value judgment. The society in which the churches were so implicated, whose defense the churches saw as in some real way part of their task, was believed to be a corrupt and threatened society. This conviction grew out of the Christian commitment of the authors and reflected their awareness that God's judgment was being experienced in the social dislocation of the era. Nor could it be claimed that the churches in America, enjoying the freedom of religion established in our founding documents, were somehow saved from subservience to the established order, or that domination of the church by its society was exclusively characteristic of Europe and its state churches. Francis P. Miller, from his vantage point as chairman of the World Student Christian Federation, put it with forcefulness:

> The plain fact is that the domestication of the Protestant community in the United States within the framework of the national culture has progressed as far as in any western land. The degradation of the American Protestant church is as complete as the degradation of any other national Protestant church. The process of degradation has been more subtle and inconspicuous, but equally devastating in its consequences for faith.[5]

The plea of the manifesto was clear: let the churches use the freedom given them by law to break the bondage into which they had stumbled. What Niebuhr called "the captive church" needed for the sake of its mission to break out of that captivity and recover its proper independence.

In Bondage to Society

That book, with its clarion call for independence, was published in 1935. As far as I can see, except for slight forays now and again, the churches are as much the captives of the culture and its working principles now as they were when the manifesto was published. The plain fact is that the church is not now against the world; the church has always been tied to the world and, in most periods of its history, has found such a relationship comfortable, flattering, and secure. It is hardly surprising that the call for independence has such a hard time being heard.

Before turning to the task of establishing clearly the fact of captivity, a word of caution is in order. To speak of the church against the world is dangerous. For this generalization can easily slide over into the theologically unsound repudiation of human history and humanity's experience. What can result is a curmudgeonly inability or refusal to affirm the worth of anything which has occurred in society. There are Christian bodies which take precisely such a position. The world is so evil that nothing ever happens in it of any positive value whatever. The only hope for the Christian is to be granted the assurance of salvation and an ultimate destiny in a fairer world. For the Christian who holds this position, there is of course nothing to be done in human society. That is God-forsaken territory better consigned to the devil and his hosts.

Such a position has at least two grave defects. One is the practical fact that hosts of sincere Christians, because of the formative power of such convictions, are self-exiled from the crucial social issues of our time. A second and more serious defect is theological. The position of those who unqualifiedly denounce the world finally involves a lack of the sense of God's grace encountered in the midst of the tangled events of our days. Such gifts, which are all about us and experienced by the sensitive daily as God's goodness, infuse life with a joy and radiance which are never to be despised. Any approach which diminishes the reality of God's presence in his world is seriously deficient so far as sustaining the Christian struggle is concerned.

Affirming God's presence, and the role of the church, in the world results, of course, in complexity rather than simplicity. Simplicity is found in either of the other viewpoints—one which condemns all that happens in the world and one which endorses and, in effect, baptizes all that goes on in the world. Those are perhaps the modern counterparts of Burckhardt's "terrible simplifiers." They would obscure the fact that Christian existence requires an anguished wrestling with complexity. For it is part of the Christian responsibility to determine when events and structures in the world are part of God's purpose and therefore properly able to claim the Christian's support and when they are events and structures which, far from being in accord with God's purpose, represent the effective denial of his purpose and therefore properly lay upon the Christian the obligation to oppose the events and structures—in short, to be against the world in order to be responsible to God. It would be the wildest folly to claim that such Christian existence is easy; but it would be folly ever to claim that our life in Christ is supposed to be easy. Careful discriminations need to be made, and the making of such discriminations is a significant part of Christian obedience.

Some rough guidelines can be suggested.[6] Albert van den Heuvel has suggested certain questions which can be put to the powers—those persons in government, business, education whose decisions determine the shape of human existence—to determine whether they have overreached themselves. Do they divide or unite? Do they focus attention on self or direct us to the needs of others? Do they claim ultimacy or are they open to amendment? Do they set us free or bind us to the past? There is nothing automatic about the application of such questions, and Christians are going to differ among themselves about the answers; but some such tests need to be used. Serious Christian involvement in the affairs of the social order depends in significant measure upon the discipline brought to the task of making discriminating judgments.

We must turn now to the task of validating a central contention of this chapter: the bondage of the churches to the existing society. The yawning chasm in this regard is between those who imagine that American society, even if it is not a perfect embodiment of the Christian way, is at least a reasonable approximation of it, and those who deny any such contention. If American society is essentially Christian, then the churches have no business being independent of such a society; their task is that of providing a buttress to uphold such a splendid social order. Such is not the position taken in these pages. Contemporary American society, like every other society, has in it elements which are in accord with God's will; and it is not jingoistic patriotism to acknowledge this and to take pride in it. At the same time, however, this society has in it much that denies the will of God as his will has been known in the biblical tradition and especially in the life and ministry of Jesus Christ. It is the task of the churches to recognize those places where the society of which they are part violates the purpose of God. The unfortunate part of captivity is that it dulls the vision of the churches to those places where society denies God's will and debases human lives. And if the churches, as the supposed spokesmen for the transcendent, forsake their independence in return for the favors of the powers-that-be, it is hardly likely that the note of judgment will be heard.

In the essay by Arthur M. Schlesinger, Sr., to which I have referred,[7] there was a suggestion that American political history has alternated between periods of liberalism and conservatism. He admitted that the reason for this is "singularly elusive" and refused to try to assign any single cause. He characterized American political history as showing the following divisions:

Liberal eras	Conservative eras
1765–1787	1787–1801
1801–1816	1816–1829
1829–1841	1841–1861
1861–1869	1869–1901
1901–1919	1919–1931
1931–1947	

The five eras of conservative rule average 18.2 years, while the liberal eras average 15 years. While it is a risky venture to try to label administrations nearer to one's own era, the risk will be run here. Without trying to argue the matter in any detail, it seems to me that the years from 1948 onward reveal a brief liberal time under Truman, eight years of conservatism under Eisenhower, eight years of generally liberal direction under Kennedy and Johnson, a return to conservatism under Nixon, and a period under Carter which mysteriously blends liberal ends and conservative means. It is also clear that because of the speeded-up nature of modern existence, no point of view lasts as long as formerly. About eight years now seems to be the maximum.

It is unnecessary to survey the entire period from 1918 on. For purposes of illustration let's choose a couple of periods and see if in those times the churches reflected the dominant trend in the larger society.[8] It should be acknowledged that in determining the major thrust of a period, it is never all one way. With this caution in mind, it is nevertheless possible to assign a major trend to a given period. The two periods I want to look at are those from 1919–1931 and the Eisenhower years, 1952–1958.

On the morning of November 11, 1918, President Woodrow Wilson took a pencil and an ordinary sheet of White House stationery and wrote out a message to the American people:

My Fellow Countrymen: The armistice was signed this morning. Everything for which America fought has been accomplished. It will now be our fortunate duty to assist by example, by sober, friendly counsel, and by material aid in the establishment of just democracy throughout the world.[9]

But the summons fell on ears deafened by many other concerns. The war was over, and the dominant desire of America was to return to normalcy. And this was done with abandon. The twenties arrived to the accompaniment of blaring jazz, flappers, flasks, rumble seats, marathon dances, flagpole sitters, and other antic activities. It was also the time when the nation gave itself to unrestrained pursuit of wealth and could not bother itself unduly with concern about the Teapot Dome, Sacco and Vanzetti, the KKK, and A. Mitchell Palmer's zealous hunt for Reds. The fervor of the nation had been exhausted in the recent war, and normalcy meant having as little to do with government as possible and rejecting responsible participation in the League of Nations. Frederick Lewis Allen, chronicler of this era, summed it up:

> The tide of events, had Wilson but known it, was turning against him. Human nature, the world over, was beginning to show a new side, as it has shown it at the end of every war in history. The compulsion for unity was gone, and division was taking its place. The compulsion for idealism was gone, and realism was in the ascendant.[10]

American society generally furnished a clear illustration of the need for a respite following the ardors of struggle and warfare.

The parallels between the society and the churches are noteworthy. The war ended with a surge of idealism on the part of the churches. On December 17, 1918, 135 prominent members of mission boards and agencies met in New York City. They began the formation of the Inter-church World Movement. Gradually, the movement generated a tremendous amount of enthusiasm. A financial goal of $336 million was adopted. Beyond the enthusiasm there was a mood of genuine confidence. "Victory in this crusade to Christianize America and the world seemed to be within reach," as Robert T. Handy summed it up in his fine book *A Christian America*.[11] But the reach fell short, and instead of a great victory, the churches confronted a smothering indifference. While the denominations supported the financial drive very well, the people seemed unconcerned. By the summer of 1920, the movement had collapsed. The churches, like the society as a whole, wanted to return to normalcy.

The period is summed up by Professor Handy:

> In addition to such particular ways of trying to maintain the familiar styles of Protestant America, there was a more general return of the normalcy of

adjusting to the main tendencies in the culture. The twenties turned out to be the decade of business, the decade of prosperity. . . . Overall, Protestantism was profiting not a little from the good times of the twenties, as is indicated by growing financial support and a marked increase in the value of church property.[12]

The conservative period from 1919 to 1931 found churches and society reflecting each other.

The years following World War II and especially those which began with the administration of Eisenhower witnessed a clear move toward conservatism. Remembering the response following World War I, this is hardly a surprising development. The exertions of war took a fantastic toll and hosts of Americans wanted nothing more than to return home, establish a family, get started on a career, and forget the world and its devastating problems. If normalcy was not the word used, it was the condition desired.

Consequently, there was a kind of euphoria engendered, which did something more than evade sticky social problems: it denied their existence. The major problem we confronted was not a society of social injustice, but a Cold War against Russian communism. Senator Joseph McCarthy created a climate of oppression and fear, recklessly shattering reputations and finding very little opposition from within the administration. If this problem is put to one side, the society was blissful and contented. It was what John Kenneth Galbraith would call "the affluent society" and hence needed nothing more than a resolute determination not to rock the boat. It was the time of conformity. We worried about "the lonely crowd" and studied the new species of "organization man" who had emerged. It was a time when you had to go along to get along, and most Americans, it seemed, wanted to get along.

The religion of those years was a strange thing indeed. For there was a "religious revival" which saw churches crowded as they had not been for a long time and church membership rise to a new high. As part of this boom, church building became a major industry. Viewed from the statistical side, religion was indeed getting along in the fifties—in some ways, it was getting along better than it ever had. Understandably, most in the churches accepted this as a happy circumstance and probably as a clear manifestation of God's obvious delight with America's churches.

Rarely have churches and society moved so neatly together. The society wanted no reminder of stubbornly persisting problems, and the churches obligingly complied by turning inward and giving themselves to enjoyment of their own prosperity. Throughout the entire society, the accent was on conformity, and in this regard the churches saw their function as that of support. The great success stories were those of Norman Vincent Peale, Fulton J. Sheen, and Billy Graham, not one of whom was on fire with a concern for social justice or had any interest in searching out the dusty corners where a complacent society had swept its dirt. It was peace of mind and soul and with God that we sought, and these three promised it. Along with peace, they offered power to secure what the society was offering everybody who really wanted it.

There was, however, a focal point of loyalty in the churches and the society. Patriotic conviction put the nation in the place of first loyalty. Partly this took place because evangelical faith had been emptied of distinctive content, and if God was unreal, the nation was visible and claimant and rushed into the vacuum. Many had a religious outlook very much like Eisenhower's, which was described by someone as a "very fervent faith in a very vague religion."[13] This explains the assessment of William Lee Miller: "The popular religious revival is closely tied to a popular patriotism, of which it is the uncritical ally: religion and Americanism, God and country, Cross and flag. The two pieties combine in much public discourse, and often the American will slide unnoticing from one to the other."[14] Society and the churches moved closer together in a process which saw the churches, intoxicated by public approval and support, forsaking the convictions which might make it necessary for them to speak in judgment.

When looked at from the point of view of those who believe that the churches, as inheritors and ideally as exemplifications of the biblical tradition of championing the cause of the poor and oppressed, the situation of dependence upon the dominant forces in society is especially melancholy. Through most of history the churches have taken on the protective coloration of the dominant interests of the society in which they exist. That dominant interest is a reflection always of the concerns of the powerful elements of the social order.

Examples of this are easily found. A particularly clear instance is found in the role of the churches in Gastonia, North Carolina. This section of the country was extremely dependent upon the mills; they provided the employment, and what prosperity the region had was due to the presence of the mills. Understandably, then, the mill owners were the powerful figures in the section; their interests tended to dominate all discussions. One interest united the owners: a firm, unbending opposition to any attempt at unionizing the mills. Bloody battles were fought and lives were lost in the struggle by the owners to keep the unions out. Liston Pope wrote a fine sociological study in religion on this situation in his book *Millhands and Preachers*. The unions were kept out, and in the effort most agencies and institutions of the community adopted the point of view of the owners.

The churches of Gastonia certainly reflected the dominant power structure of the town. More than three decades after Liston Pope's pioneering study, three social scientists, one of them a teacher of Christian social ethics who had started out as a pastor in Gastonia, went back and over a period of ten years studied the area anew. In 1953 another attempt was made to unionize the mills. Virtually every church lined up with the owners. Seven ministers of the community sent a mimeographed letter to 330 employees of the mill in Cherryville. The mailing list, as the seven ministers later admitted, had come from the mill office, although they insisted that they had paid the postage, done the mimeographing, and supplied the stationery. The letter read:

Dear Friends,

We feel that a situation threatens to arise that will disturb the good spirit and fellowship of our Community. We want you to know we are deeply concerned about your welfare. Recently we have had it called to our attention that a CIO Labor Union election is to be held in your mill Tuesday February 10. We realize that this decision rests entirely with you.

However, we feel that we would like to let you know our feelings in this matter. We are thoroughly convinced that it would be greatly to your disadvantage to have the Union to represent you. Many of the benefits and special favors which you have had would no longer be yours under the Union.

Let us urge you to get out and Vote and Vote your Conviction. We suggest that you consider this matter prayerfully before voting, and May God Guide you in your decision.

Yours in Christ's service

(signed by Seven Ministers)[15]

The lack of independence is glaringly apparent in this episode, but it is hardly warrant for churches in other areas to adopt a self-righteous stance. Any searching scrutiny, motivated by a real degree of honesty, will lead to a confession of similar capitulation to the power structure on the part of all churches. Whether found in mill town, inner city, suburbia, or academia, churches tend to sacrifice independence in exchange for the good opinion of the dominant elements.

The evidence thus far supplied—and there is much, much more of the same sort of thing—more than justifies the accuracy of the observation of Alexis de Tocqueville in the 1830s that American clergymen "allow themselves to be borne away without opposition in the current of feeling and opinion by which everything around them is carried along."[16] A modern sociologist, C. Wright Mills, updates and makes even sharper the viewpoint of his eminent predecessor:

> As a social and as a personal force, religion has become a dependent variable: It does not originate; it reacts. It does not denounce; it adapts. It does not set forth new modes of conduct and sensibility; it imitates. . . . It has become less a revitalization of the spirit in permanent tension with the world than a respectable diversion from the sourness of life.[17]

Tone down such judgments and make a place for glorious exemptions and they nevertheless remain accurate in describing the posture of American Christianity.

Affirming the World

It is in the light of this tendency that we can assess some of the more recent follies or aberrations in Christian social action. The churches in the recent past have been in captivity, some of them to the upholders of the status quo and others to the demolishers of the status quo.

The present situation is complicated because reservations have to be entered, not only against captivity to the upholders of the status quo, but against the demolishers of the status quo as well. Those whose ardent desire was to smash the establishment included a number of persons who had been part of the social gospel and Christian realism tradition. The climate of the sixties, as I have already pointed out, produced in many a mindless sanctioning of whatever radical critics of American society wanted to say and an indiscriminate willingness to espouse any technique, provided only that it did not sanction or uphold in any way the status quo. Feelings of revulsion, which may have done great credit to those who held them, were nevertheless inadequate foundations for effective social policy. The sixties, while right in their general direction, exhibited some incredibly inept social strategies. Too often the heart went without the head, and such a condition is always a prelude to sad ineffectiveness.

It seems to me that the independence for which I am pleading can never be achieved without the clear and explicit repudiation of our recent flirtation with the secular and with worldliness. Both terms are used but behind them lies a single reality.

Before the new enthusiasm toward the secular and worldly could be accepted with total commitment, it was necessary to prepare the way. The terms had to be given new meaning, because as formerly used they stood for forces in opposition to Christian faith and practice. It took some rather skilled—and, I believe, tortuous—redefining to accomplish this purpose.

The changed status of the secular can well be considered one of the great comebacks of our era. John C. Bennett, writing in 1936 in *Christianity—and our World*, defined secularism as

> that characteristic of our world according to which life is organized apart from God, as though God did not exist.... From a religious point of view it means that the highest objects of devotion are human ideals and human causes which emerge in the social process.[18]

So changing are theological fads that if you skip no more than two and a half decades, you will find the secular ensconced in a place of honor. To be secular is evidently what we should have been after all. The titles bounce out of my shelves: *The Secular City, The Secular Meaning of the Gospel, The Secular Christ, Secular Christianity, Secular Impact*—and those are only the titles immediately visible to me! All our concern spent in thinking that the secular somehow was an adversary to overcome was so much wasted energy. All we had to do was ride into the glamorous and glistening city and see its manifold wonders.

Once again, it is important to make a careful distinction. If by secular is meant a concern on the part of religious institutions for the affairs of human society, then that can be given nothing but wholehearted approval. Such a concern is manifestly a need of the churches and society today. As the term is often used, especially by some of its less careful and more zealous devotees, it indicates not so much a belief that the churches need to be involved in such issues as a conviction of almost complacent approval of what a secular society has achieved. It is, after all, one thing to be "secular" in terms of working diligently at the concerns of the public sector; it is quite another matter to be "secular" in terms of approval of what society has produced. Sometimes, reading the enthusiastic affirmations of addicts of the secular in the sixties, one had the feeling that such persons were as far removed from any kind of fundamental attack on society's wrongs as were those who rejected social involvement because they believed such actions to be invalid as expressions of Christian existence. Those who would condemn secular out of hand and those who affirm it without reservation end up partners in social complacency.

At the same time we were embellishing the image of the secular, we were polishing up the luster of worldliness. This was a bit more difficult, because the New Testament seemed to imply that the worldly was rather definitely an enemy to be wrestled with. But this did not daunt us for very long.

Two things were required. The world had to be given a status that would make it attractive. Some found a way to do so in the prison correspondence of Dietrich Bonhoeffer. The letter of June 8, 1944, is pivotal. It is a puzzling bit of correspondence which I confess I find hard to understand. It blends perceptive insight with what seems to me to be wild exaggeration. He began with a sober historical description:

> The movement beginning about the thirteenth century . . . towards the autonomy of man . . . has in our time reached a certain completion. Man has learned to cope with all questions of importance without recourse to God as a working hypothesis. . . . As in the scientific field, so in human

affairs generally, what we call "God" is being more and more edged out of life, losing more and more ground.[19]

While I would want to say "man *thinks* he has learned to cope," the words are accurate enough as a description. But then Bonhoeffer makes the amazing assertion that this process he has sketched is proof that the world has come of age!

And this assertion is what is so hard to understand. The man who made this judgment was himself in prison; he had been put there at the hands of a regime of monstrous evil; he was part of a people who, despite fantastic expertise in scientific and technological areas, had been taken captive by a vicious regime; millions of Jews had been liquidated by this same regime; the world had been plunged into a hideous nightmare of destruction and killing; and he himself had wrestled with his Christian conscience and finally determined that he had to share in the plot to assassinate Hitler. Yet in that setting he could talk of a world come of age! If language has any precision, that is a strange way to talk. For to "come of age" surely means that one has reached a level of maturity so that one can be trusted to make decisions for oneself with a confident assurance that the decisions will be both responsible and constructive. If coming of age, as the term is generally used, does not mean this, I do not know what it means. And if that is indeed the meaning of the phrase "world come of age," it is about the last judgment to be applied to our world.

What a manifestation of the vacuity of modern theology that it attempted to build an industry on the exegesis of fragmentary pieces of correspondence! This takes nothing from Bonhoeffer's greatness either as man or as theologian; it is simply a caution against erecting vast structures on slender and questionable foundations. This contention that the world has come of age is given biting treatment by Jacques Ellul. He writes:

> It is time to close ranks: man is coming of age. Until 1900 man walked on all fours, now he walks upright. What am I saying, upright? Since 1945 he even has little wings, he walks three inches off the ground.... Now, at last, humanity has rid itself of its taboos. It no longer believes it has a father, there is no more God in heaven to turn to, man is turning his back on all this childishness, and *by this very act,* he is coming of age.[20]

If the announcement that the world has come of age did not suffice, any remaining stigma in worldliness could be removed by a second action. An adjective—"holy"—was placed in front of the noun—"worldliness"—neatly permitting us to be worldly and to feel pious at the same time.

It is, incidentally, interesting to note how exquisitely sensitive some theologians were to sin in the Christian community and how utterly unable they were to see sin in the secular society. Instead of recognizing that society, like our human nature, mixes misery and grandeur, it seemed to be essential to affirm the wonderful goodness of the secular and worldly and to make them shine brighter by making the churches look more dismal. A strange and sick self-loathing, which finally hampered any clarity of insight about the actual situation of the world, characterized some of those who affirmed the world.

If what I have been contending is accurate, the strangest slogan of all would have to be: "The world must write the agenda for the church." It is dazzling to think about that: the world, which gives no attention to Scripture, lives without the discipline of liturgy, cares nothing for the lordship of Jesus Christ, invokes God only in profanity— that world is to determine the agenda for the believing community! If ever a slogan demonstrated the bankruptcy of the Christian community, that one surely does. We who try to live informed by the biblical tradition, nourished by worship, obedient in intention to the lordship of Christ, open to the leading of the Spirit, know how hard it is to find the will of God in the tangled events of our common life. Evidently we have wasted our energy. It is all there to be found out in the world. Up against such an assertion, Alice in Wonderland, believing seven impossible things before breakfast, was a real skeptic.

The recovery of the independence of the churches requires a firm and clear repudiation of the dead ends which have been followed in a futile and often pathetic quest for relevance. What is needed is an approach which affirms the world as the arena of our witness but denies the world as the source of our direction. Theological poise is required which will give the world our best effort but depend upon our life in God and the Christian community for the source of our basic insights into the responses appropriate for Christians. No ignoring of the turbulent movements of our day can be permitted, but all such movements need discerning evaluation by Christians, utilizing all possible insights from sociology, political science, economics, and all other relevant disciplines, but never forgetting that such areas of knowledge are to aid in, and not simply to substitute for, a theological assessment which remains the unique task of the Christian churches.

The Root of Independence

The independence for which this chapter pleads is not sought for the sake of the welfare of the churches; it is sought because it seems to me to be a position essential for effectiveness in social witness. If the churches are to fulfill their mandate and be the voices for the weak, the poor, the oppressed, they dare not be so tied to the power structure that the sound of judgment is stifled. Such independence requires, of course, a theological stance which has strength and vigor. It is the kind of vital theology which is behind the incisive words of P. T. Forsyth in describing the stance of the churches: "She faced the world with a boon but also a demand. . . . She served a world she would not obey, in the name of a mastery it could neither confer nor withstand. She did not lead the world, nor echo it; she confronted it."[21] Effective social Christianity awaits that kind of apostolic independence.

It is, of course, easy enough to call for independence of the churches over against the society. It is not so easy to indicate what this involves for the churches. Clearly, it will involve significant readjustments of both thought and practice. The churches, if they are to recover independence, will have to renounce certain aspects of past thought and practice.

3

Churches and the
Passing of Christendom

When *The Church Against the World* was first published, it was reviewed by Charles Clayton Morrison in *The Christian Century Pulpit*. He acknowledged that attaining independence was a laudable objective, but complained that the authors did not "constructively define the kind of church which will emerge if their call to independence is heeded." His colleague, W. E. Garrison, reviewing the book in *The Christian Century,* asserted that the authors had sounded a "trumpet call to nothing in particular."[1] There is validity in such criticism, although the basic purpose of the book was not to sketch out details; it was, rather, to awaken a complacent Christian community to awareness of its real condition. The need to trace the implications of the thesis remains.

If independence of the churches is as important as claimed, it is essential to try to indicate both the nature of such churches and the cost in bringing such churches into being. What follows in this and the next two chapters is an endeavor to think through the implications of the call for independence in the setting of the Christian community today. It is important to stress that these pages arise out of the specific situation. It is that of Christians puzzled about what took place in the sixties, uncomfortable about some of

51

the tendencies of the seventies, and consequently not at all sure what should be done in the eighties.

Nostalgia for Christendom

There are many difficulties encountered in preparing for effective Christian social action in the immediate future. Perhaps nothing is more difficult than the required readjustment in outlook, for this involves the abandonment of deeply cherished convictions about the possibility of Christianizing the social order, to use a phrase from Rauschenbusch. Perceptive observers have been saying for some time that the era of Christendom is over. To recognize that condition and yet not be shattered by a failure of nerve is one of the significant challenges now facing Christians.

It won't be an easy matter to avoid a failure of nerve. Christendom, as reality or dream, has figured very largely in the outlook of Christian groups. While premature assurance of the reality of Christendom has sometimes contributed to complacency, the possibility of bringing such an ordering of society into existence has generated a tremendous outpouring of social action and concern. It would therefore be an unwise strategy not to take seriously the meaning of the passing of Christendom.

It will be necessary to deal, as helpfully as possible, with the revisions of outlook and strategy called for by the end of Christendom, but that is not the first task confronted. The realization that Christendom has come to an end and that we have entered into a very different kind of existence has not by any means penetrated into the consciousness of the churches and their members. Of course, scholars have been saying for some time that Christendom is over, but the acceptance of this contention is tardy. The illusion of Christendom has been cherished, and so the shattering of the illusion is a high priority need in Christian social strategy.

There is no doubt that Christendom embodied a glowing ideal in the hearts of believers. The idea of a society imbued with Christian standards in every relation of life is enough to kindle the hearts and minds of all who take faith with seriousness. If God is the sovereign Creator and Sustainer of all existence, what could be more natural and desirable than that God should control all aspects of human existence? In this vision, no area of life was not responsible to the

Christian institution. So completely did the church dominate the society that all persons were to be counted among its members, and many of the rights of persons were dependent upon membership in the Christian community. This was true not only of personal existence; it was true in some measure of corporate existence as well. Business and government were hardly to be carried on as autonomous enterprises. They, too, were subject to the control of the church. Because of the tremendous power held by the church, an element of coercion entered in, in terms of forcing people into membership and institutions into conformity with the church's understanding of what God required. Rarely was the control total, but there were periods when such a degree was closely approached. And this Christendom remained as a kind of ideal or goal. It should be said, in passing, that not only was this the goal of much Catholic social theory, but also in some ways it is not wholly different from the goal of the social gospel movement within Protestantism in America.

There is considerable difficulty in accepting the fact that Christendom is truly over. Intellectually, of course, the facts can be absorbed, if for no other reason than that they are clear and forceful. But emotionally there remains a feeling that the order of Christendom is what *should* be the case. Perhaps it has passed from the scene, but maybe it can be restored in some measure—this has been the mood of many in the churches.

It is necessary to take this feeling seriously into account in any attempt to frame a social strategy for the future. The hold of this ideal on the hearts of believers remains very strong, and a moment should be taken to indicate some of the reasons for the persistence of this mood.

In addition to the lingering nostalgia for the medieval structure, there is the fact that this ordering of all existence was very much part of the Puritan goal for this country. No matter how the Puritan influence is assessed now, the outlook has been a strong formative influence in American religious life and indeed in American life generally. The Puritans were animated by a clear goal. They intended to establish on these shores a society governed in all essential details by standards derived from the Bible. It would be a "city upon a hill." It would be in truth a holy commonwealth in which true churches would guide with firmness the life of individuals and society. "The early Puritans," Robert T. Handy writes, "forcefully stated their vision of Zion in America, and sought to make it visible. Declaring that the Bible set forth the basic laws for individual and family, church and nation, they endeavored to follow them in detail."[2] The zealous attempt of the Puritans did not finally succeed; but, like the medieval vision, the Puritan commonwealth has always remained a tantalizing if elusive goal of American religion.

Not only is the hold of the ideal of Christendom to be found in the Puritan experience, but also it is firmly rooted in the soil of American religious thought. A conversionist or transformationist motif has always bulked large in theological thought in America.

When H. Richard Niebuhr set out the typologies for the different understandings held by Christians of the relation between Christ and culture, he enumerated five such types: Christ against culture, the Christ of culture, Christ above culture, Christ and culture in paradox, and Christ the transformer of culture.[3] It is not hard to choose among the five the one which most clearly accords with the convictions and hopes of those in the tradition of either the social gospel or Christian realism.

The social gospel tradition was deeply committed to the transformationist motif. From its inception it was a movement which took seriously the possibility that the structures of the social order could be transformed by the power of Christian commitment until the kingdom of God was made visible and dominant. There was in the thought of Rauschenbusch himself a certain ambiguity. With part of his being he affirmed that the kingdom was to come by way of development and specifically noted that

> we must shift from catastrophe to development. Since the first century the divine Logos has taught us the universality of Law, and we must apply it to the development of the Kingdom of God. It is the untaught and pagan mind which sees God's presence only in miraculous and thundering action; the more Christian our intellect becomes, the more we see God in growth.[4]

Quickly, however, that developmental emphasis is qualified by noting that the "coming of the Kingdom of God will not be by peaceful development only, but by conflict with the Kingdom of Evil. We should estimate the power of sin too lightly if we forecast a smooth road. Nor does the insistence on continuous development eliminate the possibility and value of catastrophes."[5] This uncertainty does not really cancel the basic point: the social gospel believed that the structures of the social order were capable of being transformed, either through orderly development or by cataclysmic upheaval. If this confidence was the source of dangerous illusions in the social gospel tradition, it was likewise the source of a splendid dynamic.

The followers of Reinhold Niebuhr, the Christian realists, repudiated the extravagant hopes of the social gospel. But they, too, were committed to the transformationist motif. They did not expect such wholesale transformations, but they did believe in the power of Christian effort to effect significant changes in the social order. Even Reinhold Niebuhr, despite his trenchant criticisms of the false optimism of the social gospel, cautioned against undue limiting of what could be accomplished. Because so much of his writing was polemical in nature, it is easy to lose sight of the real accomplishments he believed achievable in social reform. His determination not to let achievements, no matter how real, become sources of complacency led him to expend most of his energy in deflating pretensions. "An optimism which depends upon the hope of the complete realization of our highest ideals in history is bound to suffer ultimate disillusionment. All such optimistic illusions have resulted in such a fate throughout history."[6] Such pronouncements are familiar bits of Niebuhrian polemics. It should also be noted, however, that he went on to affirm that "the beauty and meaning of human life are partially revealed in ideals and aspirations which transcend all possibilities of achievement in history. They may be [and these are the important words] approximated and each approximation may lead to further visions."[7] Nothing more than this needs to be claimed here. One suspects that behind Christian realism, almost as much as behind social gospel idealism, there has always lurked a wistful yearning for the lost glory of Christendom and that in this regard the two traditions are not as far apart as we sometimes assume.

It is against this background—the medieval ideal, the Puritan zeal for a Christian America, the transformationist motif—that we can understand the persistence of the idea of Christendom. If repudiated in academia, it lives on in the stubborn insistence of many that this is "a Christian nation." After all, our coins proclaim this and our politicians in every peroration affirm it. If national existence is not examined too closely, it comforts citizens to think that, no matter how serious our problems, we are still somewhat unique in being a Christian people. Thus does innocence persist, untroubled by anything so inconvenient as a fact.

Confronting the Death of Christendom

But the illusion must finally be abandoned. What is left of Christendom is a nostalgic memory. "Vestigial scars, medallia, and figures of speech recalling the grand alliance," writes Stephen Crites, "will doubtless continue for some time to adhere to both church and culture. Indeed, most Christians are finding it hard to reconcile themselves to their disestablishment."[8] The move toward this disestablishment is painful for religious groups in this country. If such a transition is to be made successfully, there must be clarity regarding the nature of religious organizations which are active in our midst.

In terms of the European origin of most of our religious beliefs and practices, two forms of organization were given most of the attention. One was the church. The other was the sect. Yet in actual fact neither of these terms properly described the religious organizations which have dominated the American scene.

The dominant form among us has been the denomination. Both the origin and the genius of this type of religious organization have been given cogent exposition by Winthrop S. Hudson. He made clear in a famous essay that denominationalism, while it reached its fullest development on these shores, originated among the Dissenting deputies in seventeenth-century England. Instead of looking upon denominationalism as a scandalous sign of our divided condition, he argues that denominationalism is a "basis for ecumenicity." In developing his high view of denominational Christianity, Professor Hudson writes:

> Denominationalism is the opposite of sectarianism. The word "denomina-tion" implies that the group referred to is but one member of a larger group, called or denominated by a particular name. The basic contention of the denominational theory of the church is that the true church is not to be identified in any exclusive sense with any particular ecclesiastical institution. . . . Yet all denominations recognize their responsibility for the whole of society and they expect to cooperate in freedom and mutual respect with other denominations in discharging that responsibility.[9]

This essay has had an important effect in developing a new attitude toward denominationalism.

There is no doubt that this denominational concept of the way in which to organize for Christian work illumines the American scene. Nor can there be any doubt that this was a means by which the colonists were enabled to make a concerted attack on the religious indifference of the early settlers. Since so much has been written to the effect that denominationalism represents a tragic aberration, denying by its existence the unity we so badly need, it is salutary to be reminded that the denominational form of churches manifested the qualities essential for effective functioning in the new environment and may well continue to serve this objective in our day.

The denomination, then, represents the way in which the religious bodies organized for Christian mission on these shores. The denomination operated on the basis of certain convictions shared by neither the church nor the sect. The case for denominationalism, as outlined by Professor Hudson in his *American Protestantism*, rests upon six characteristics. First, the denominations accepted the inevitability of different ways of organizing religious bodies, a condition known even in the New Testament. Second, these differences, while they are not ultimate, are nevertheless important. Third, the differences which exist can lead to fruitful discussion and out of such sharing may come a fuller understanding of the truth. Fourth, recognizing that no church has a corner on God's truth, no single structure can ever represent the true church of Christ. Fifth, the different organizations and even the differing interpretations of doctrine do not annul the unity believers have in Jesus Christ. And, sixth, the fact of separation is not of itself an indication of schism.[10] Out of such operating convictions the denominationalism with which we are familiar has evolved.

These operating convictions distinguish the denomination from either church or sect. But at this point it is necessary to move back and relate what has been set forth to the reality of the end of Christendom. What I suggest is that the denomination, while it differs from church and sect, nevertheless shows at various times characteristics which are classically associated with the church-type or the sect-type. In terms of the concern of these pages, it seems that the churchly ideal of Christendom takes on new life among the denominations in periods when things seem to be going well for Christian enterprises. And, on the other hand, in periods when things are going badly, the denominations are likely to take on some of the characteristics of the sect-type.

Before this phenomenon can be looked at in detail, we need to be clear about the marks of the church and the sect. To do this, we go back to Ernst Troeltsch and his classic descriptions.

The church-type and the sect-type have distinctive marks and each has both assets and liabilities. "The Church," Troeltsch said, "desires to cover the whole life of humanity. The sects, on the other hand, are comparatively small groups; they aspire after personal inward perfection, and they aim at a direct personal fellowship between the members of each group."[11] The church becomes a part of the existing order of society, both stabilizing and determining the shape of that social order. In the process the church invariably becomes dependent upon the upper classes. The sect, on the contrary, maintains an attitude of detachment, indifference, or hostility toward the society.

The denomination is clearly a new structure which has in it elements of both the church and the sect. The thesis I want to suggest is that in periods of relative Christian effectiveness, when there are some fairly impressive successes to which to point, the denomination begins to think in churchly terms and the ghostly reality of Christendom once again floats across the horizon. The hope is renewed that perhaps the old dream can take on new substance and maybe the bold venture can be brought off. Ours is not such a period. Accordingly, it is now necessary for the denominations to divest themselves of any lingering dream of Christendom and move in the direction of what can be called a more sectarian strategy in their functioning.

Let me indicate, in quick and summary fashion, some of the characteristics which will mark this new denominationalism. First, it will accept a continuing involvement in the struggles of the social order. It recognizes that the purity achieved by flight is a denial of faith, and that grace is seen not in the gift of purity but in the gift of forgiveness.

Second, the denominations, in seeking separation from identification with the wielders of power, pursue this course not for the sake of their purity but for the sake of effective witness in and to the world.

By maintaining separation from the powerful and oppressive, the churches can be allied with the poor and oppressed and see with greater penetration and clarity the iniquities of which power is invariably guilty.

Third, the new denominationalism manifests an unremitting concern to shape its own life in such fashion as to provide a paradigm of what divine ruling would be. Lewis Mudge has sought a way to bridge the gulf between church and sect. What he urged is a group of

> men and women who know the biblical tradition and celebrate it. Sociologically speaking, such a company of persons is bound today to function as something of a "sect," or at least as an organized religious minority. From this status there is no escape if the tradition is taken seriously. . . .
>
> But we are discovering that the *content* of this tradition demands that we see ourselves not as persons saved out of a fallen world, but rather as persons called to be *that very world reconstituted as the social space, and therefore as the worldly reality of God's rule.*[12]

Thus the new denominationalism will have at its center a concern for the world God loves.

Fourth, the new denominationalism, no longer supinely tied to the "principalities and powers," will be willing to work in behalf of a new ordering of society. It will see its role as akin to that of Jeremiah "to pluck up and to break down, to destroy and to overthrow, to build and to plant" (Jeremiah 1:10). It will not see peace and quiet as the sure marks of God's presence but will see that the Divine breaks into history and manifests his presence in the overthrowing of arrogant oppressors. There will be no pious cry of "Peace, peace, when there is no peace" (Jeremiah 6:14) or "Justice, justice, when there is no justice." The churches will be under no tender-minded illusion that entrenched power yields to lofty sentiments; they will know that power structures yield only to moral insight and passion effectively directed to appropriate spots. The churches will have to be ready to use power but also careful to determine the utilization of such power, not in accord with the strategies of other groups, but in accord with the understanding of power and its potential for good or evil which arises out of Christian faith.

Such churches will accept the end of Christendom and will do so with a sense, not that something has been lost, but that a new opportunity has been offered. Rightly understood and accepted, the end of Christendom gives the churches a unique chance to recover the integrity and authenticity lost in surrendering to society the determination of the proper role for God's people. The end of Christendom is the Exodus for God's people in this day. It is the setting which makes possible our liberation into integrity.

A New Strategy

Suppose churches took seriously the opportunity provided by this understanding of their role. How would they actually function in regard to bringing about social change? There are models to indicate how social Christianity might operate in light of this more sectarian understanding of denominationalism.

This model is taken from Garry Wills's account of the movement for women's suffrage. His article centers on the work of a remarkable woman, Harriot Stanton Blatch, daughter of the founder of the movement. Returning from England in 1906, she found the movement "had faded to a murmur and a tinkle amid teacups."[13] She set about to change all that. The first task was to change the partisans of the movement. Sensitive to the charge by critics that the movement made them unladylike, the women had become paragons of all that ladies were supposed to be—and, in the process, utterly irrelevant. It was a movement, said Mrs. Blatch, which "bored its adherents and repelled its opponents."[14] One year she called a parade of the women but found that many considered marching to be undignified and hence rode. The next year the rule was clear: only those willing to walk could participate; and for those who did not know how to walk, a physical education teacher would be hired to train them. Turning to politics, she determined that if she and her colleagues could not elect public officials sympathetic to the cause, they could defeat those antagonistic to it. And this they set out to do, and in the long run they succeeded. What was done in this cause is a model for Christian social action tactics in the eighties.

The type of Christian social action, needed as a tactic in the uncertain situation of the future, is indicated in some of Garry Wills's comments. He said:

The women had discovered an important truth about American politics. Creative change does not come about by the calm and open discussion of an issue on its merits, leading to a "verdict" by the judicious public. What happens is quite different: an intransigent minority makes a nuisance of itself until most of the public says, "All right, give them what they want, shut them up." [15]

What then happens is interesting. The new enactment becomes part of the Establishment and is accepted and even honored, credit often being taken for it by the same politicians who most conspicuously and vociferously opposed it.

At the center of this type of tactic is an awareness of varying roles within the social order. A vital society needs the politician and the prophet, and it needs to understand that the two rarely if ever live in the same skin. This is not to say that the prophet is good, the politician bad; it is to recognize that the roles are important but never identical. Great mischief results when we try to make politicians out of prophets or prophets out of politicians.

The role of the politician is clear. "Politicians do not bring about change. Their effort, very useful in its way, is to prevent change—to slow it down, blunt it, absorb it. That is why they need such persistent prodding before they will respond at all." [16] Let me stress again: this is an honorable and essential role in our society which Christians should be encouraged to undertake.

But what we do not always see so clearly is that the prophet is essential in a prophetic role but disastrous when put in the role of a power-broker. For the very qualities which make an effective prophet produce a disastrous politician. Mr. Wills is clearly right:

> It is fortunate that such people cannot trade their way into power, since they would make the worst of all possible rulers. They are rigid and unyielding, proud and self-righteous; they set impossibly high standards for the rest of us. They make us appreciate the purely political virtues of compromise, easily pleased vanity, and mediocre expectation—the virtues that make for continuity in society. . . . The prophet's gifts are not those of the king. [17]

This example provides, I believe, a way of functioning that will perhaps be somewhat different from the operating assumptions either of social gospel idealism or of Christian realism. Over against at least some types of social gospel idealism, it will have no illusions that change can be produced without its advocates becoming nuisances. Since disestablishment will have removed them from their places as buttresses of the status quo, Christian bodies will not be hindered in expressing radical criticisms of the society in behalf of the poor and the voiceless. No longer having such heavy emotional— and, to be quite honest about it, material—holdings in the existing society, they will be able to operate with greater freedom and a more passionate concern for justice. It is from this small minority that there will come the fundamental questions, the probing analyses, the passionate protests, and, when the occasion is right, the forthright action which will in some measure be an instrument of significant social change.

But this tactic will not please all the adherents of Christian realism. There has been, in much of the writing by Christian realists, a call for Christian bodies to be willing to assume the responsibilities of power itself. Not content with protest for its own sake, the demand has been voiced that there be willingness to do more than issue high-sounding goals and ideals; there needs to be a readiness on the part of Christian bodies to show how the ideal is to be implemented and, if necessary, not to be reluctant to take over administration of social goals. This is a helpful word, and when it cautions against the persistent Christian temptation to imagine that the verbal statement of the ideal is tantamount to the fulfillment of our responsibility, it is a needed and wholesome word. But if what has been said about independence, the end of Christendom, the fact of disestablishment, has validity, then serious questions must be raised. Perhaps the actual wielding of power is not what Christian bodies should be about. Perhaps the real task of churches, as their real contribution to the society of which they are part, is precisely to stand off from the actual operation, not in order to keep hands clean, but in order to keep vision clear.

Is the position sketched out thus far in this book a real possibility for the churches? It would be pleasant to cast off restraint and affirm this to be a real possibility. I suspect, however, that such would not be an honest reply. This sort of position will be possible for a minority within the churches, but this is not, in my opinion, cause for discouragement or excuse for passivity. There may come into being— and the possibilities of this are good—a group who will function within the churches much as the Catholic Workers and Dorothy Day have functioned within the Roman Catholic Church. Like that intrepid group, those who are willing to leave snug harbors and head for open seas will remain responsible and dedicated sons and daughters of the churches. There will be no flight into Establishment complacency or into revolutionary destruction. The way will be the harder one: to stand within the life of the organized religious communities, to share in the disciplines of that life in Word and worship, to accept a real part in the privilege of bearing one another's burdens, to affirm a sense of Christian solidarity with fellow believers with whom there are real differences on many issues. Nothing about what is here sketched in rudimentary fashion is easy. But unless signs are quite misleading, there is no chance that Christian mission in the eighties will be easy.

Thus far we have tried to explore our present plight, taking a look back at the sixties, around at the seventies, and ahead to the eighties. Essential in preparation, we have said, is the recovery of independence and the recognition that Christendom has passed from the scene. A troublesome question haunts us: What will such a changed estimate of our situation do to the power of the churches? The question must be faced, and the next chapter will try to explore the kind of power this new thrust would require.

4

The Power of Weakness and the Weakness of Power

All men, Bertrand Russell said, would like to be God; some few find it difficult to admit the impossibility.[1] If this yearning to be God is a temptation experienced to some degree by all persons, it is an especially sharp temptation for believers in the Christian community. Since the churches see their role as that of speaking *for* God, it is ever so easy to slip across the line and see the role as that of speaking *as* God. From this confusion flow the consequences of unwarranted craving for power and the folly of judging the effectiveness of mission in terms of the degree of worldly power exercised by Christian bodies. The result, visible in most eras of history, is a serious distortion of the function of religious bodies.

Ambivalence About Power

A puzzling situation is confronted when we begin to explore the ramifications of power and churches. There is hardly anything which is potentially more upsetting to our conventional ways of thinking than the gospel's understanding of power. At the same time, however, it is apparent that the churches have been uncommonly successful in keeping this revolutionary potential from becoming actual. The insight of Christian faith, as represented in the biblical tradition, is

65

that what the world considers strength is really weakness; and what the world looks upon as weakness is truly power. Paul Lehmann has summed up this radical Christian insight in his assertion that Jesus opposed the weakness of power by the power of weakness.[2]

Power is a thorny and vexing issue, but it cannot be permanently dodged. When it comes to dealing with power, however, religious institutions betray a strange uneasiness. Having failed to develop an outlook which permits them to wield power and yet to be aware of the peril of its possession, churches have been singularly ineffectual. Ambivalence about power is a persisting characteristic of Christian thought.

In retrospect we can see that a wrong turn was taken by Christian forces a long time ago. When Constantine made Christianity the official religion of the empire and when as a result religious institutions gradually gathered great power, both temporal and spiritual, a process started which has continued virtually unabated to this day. Having had a taste of power, the churches were reluctant ever to relinquish it and most of the time sought avidly to gain greater amounts of it. It has not mattered whether the churches were strong or weak; they remained in either condition enamored of power. If power was within their grasp, they felt it only right to wield it. If they did not have it, they spent time either yearning for it or serving those who had it.

A situation like this, having prevailed for a long time, is not going to be overcome easily or quickly. Protest groups, urging that it is inappropriate for churches to have or seek such power, have appeared from time to time. Rarely, however, were such groups able to persuade the larger body of the correctness of their contention and they moved finally to the edges of the community, steadfast in their witness but slight in their impact. The time has come for the churches to give new attention to the issue of power, bringing to bear insights from the Bible and Christian thought so that the understanding of power may be illumined not so much by society's opinions as by the churches' own sources of illumination.

The difficulty of the task should not be underestimated. What happened a long time ago with Constantine may have been an error, but it is important to realize that the overcoming of the error is extremely difficult because the error has not only caused distortion but also has conferred a host of benefits. It is not possible to be totally indifferent to those benefits, and certainly we can't expect to be delivered completely from the human penchant to achieve power, prestige, and all the other things that flow from special preference. A fresh beginning is only likely if we can turn with new seriousness to what the biblical tradition implies on this issue. It would be folly and presumption to claim that even this attempt to think through the issue of power will be exempt from the tendency, so often seen, of trying to bend the biblical tradition to fit into some preconceived mold. What can be affirmed is that the attempt is made by one who has felt the strong lure of the vision of a society in which power is exercised by the spiritual forces. It is the impact of recent history which has made revision of outlook necessary.

This venture may prepare the way for the second step which needs to be taken. This will involve a critical look at what churches are doing in relating to the power structures of our day. This task can be appropriately undertaken only by bearing in mind the argument thus far in these pages. This argument has suggested that there is need, in looking toward effective social witness in the eighties, for a new independence of the religious bodies and an acceptance of the reality of the end of Christendom and the fact of a "second disestablishment."[3] A situation of independence and disestablishment has clear implications for the way in which the churches understand their functioning in a world of power struggles.

Power and Our Image of God

It is not surprising that Christians should be enamored of power. From our earliest experiences of Christian life and worship, we are surrounded with emphases that make power a distinctive element of our religious outlook. With consistent emphasis we are taught to think of God in terms of power; he is *almighty* God. In much of our liturgical expression, Jesus is not the humble figure of New Testament portrayal; he is "King of Kings and Lord of Lords." The intention at this point is not to assess whether such emphases are true or false, helpful or harmful, but only to note how pervasive such assertions are.

Liturgy clearly expresses this adulation of power. Look casually through any standard hymnal and you will be impressed by this. So many of the hymns sound this note of power. Being powerful is what God means in conventional piety. "We Sing the Mighty Power of God," "God of Our Fathers, Whose Almighty Hand," "God the Omnipotent," "Praise to the Lord, the Almighty," "Come, Thou Almighty King," "All Hail the Power of Jesus' Name," "Holy, Holy, Holy, Lord God Almighty"—and there are many others. Such hymns shape religious outlooks. This is especially true in Protestant worship because, as Erik Routley has pointed out, in this branch of the church the hymns are the liturgy. It requires little reflection to realize that over a period of time such hymns prepare people to associate power with God.

One of the characteristics of great power is a capacity to be impervious to suffering. Power does not suffer; power may cause suffering by imposing itself on others; but the nature of power is such that the one who has it acts instead of being acted upon. A quality of impassibility is therefore characteristic of power.

It is this quality which is often reflected in the popular religious art depicting Jesus. The portrait by Sallman is a good illustration of this. The face of Jesus is smooth and unlined; the brow has no creases of care; there is no indication that this is one "despised and rejected of men, a man of sorrows," but rather one singularly untroubled by any of the suffering experienced in life. Serenity is what comes to mind, a serenity not of a deep inner peace achieved in the midst of struggle and anguish, but the serenity achieved by exemption from such experiences.

A clear contrast is seen in the depictions of Jesus by Roualt. These are hardly popular, because they vividly show a man torn apart by burdens too heavy to be borne. To look at such portrayals is to see the anguish that the sin and suffering of people bring upon him; this is no impervious man but one who felt with inexpressible intensity the burden and brokenness of the world. "Impassibility" would be the last word to link with such a figure.

In common with much in Christian theological thought, the emphasis on God as power, incapable of suffering because of what was called his impassibility, came from the Greek philosophical heritage. The Greeks from a very early time invested the gods with qualities strikingly in contrast to those of humans. What humans did only by dint of great effort the gods did easily. They possessed powers whose very nature included a capacity to accomplish certain ends and to do so without stress or strain.

What was a dominant motif in Greek thought about God became a powerful current in Christian theology through Augustine. Under Greek influence, Augustine decided that whatever did not change was superior to what experienced change, and therefore he placed in the stream of Christian thought the conviction that God could not change. Certainly, God could not suffer and hence was soon looked upon as impassible. In thus exalting God's power, Augustine inadvertently lost sight of more basic attributes.

Perhaps because of a belief that the powerful could be brought under spiritual control only by the imposition of greater power, Christian thought developed its idea of God's power not as something different from worldly power but simply greater than such power. Jürgen Moltmann has said:

> There are good historical grounds for arguing that while the Christian church gained the ancient world with its proclamation of God, from Justinian at the latest the Caesars conquered in the church. We can see this in the concept of God in the fact that God was now understood in terms of the image of the Egyptian pharaohs, the Persian kings and the Roman emperors. The church bestowed on God those attributes which formerly belonged exclusively to the Caesar. In so doing it certainly brought the Caesars under the authority of God, in a critical sense, but at the same time it formulated the authority of God in terms of the image of the Caesars, in an affirmative sense. In the great period of the origin of theistic philosophy and theology, which essentially led to Islam, thought took three main lines: 1. God in the image of the imperial ruler; 2. God in the image of the personification of moral energy; 3. God in the image of the final principle of philosophy. But measured by the origin of Christian faith in the crucified Christ, these three images are idols.[4]

It is precisely these idolatries which need to be repudiated, in order to rid our minds of ideas of God's power which are at variance with his actual way of dealing with us.

Instead of holding in the center of our thought of God the reality of his gracious dealing with us, we fell into what Geddes MacGregor called "dynamolatry."[5] "I am convinced," he said, "that we must learn to revolutionize our thinking about God in such a way that the old models of power-worship are thoroughly undermined so that they may give place to a radically new vision of God."[6] This new vision of God which MacGregor feels is needed will recognize that

> the only kind of power that God can intelligibly be said to exercise is whatever power love can be said to exercise. As God is incapable of any envy, so he is incapable of wantonness. Having no "worlds to conquer," no possible "ambition" (if one may so speak), he can . . . go only one way, the way of self-diminishment, which is the way of love. So he comes in meekness because he *is* meek, in humility because he *is* humble. Yet that meekness, that humility, is the greatest possible moral splendor and the greatest of all power.[7]

Many years ago John Oman argued with impressive insight that we can remain faithful to the biblical tradition only when we note the gracious way in which God deals with us. In his book *Grace and Personality*, Oman contended that the view of God's working which stressed his irresistible might

> needs to be revised, and that the way of doing it is not to lay down *à priori* regulations, argued from the bare idea of omnipotence, but, instead, to consider God's actual way of dealing with His children. When we do so, we see that the argument from His omnipotence is an assumption based on the mere naked idea of absolute force and in no way concerned with the notion of God as Father: for, if in all things He deals with us as a Father, His grace cannot be thus divorced from His working in nature and ordinary history.[8]

He goes on to suggest, in a vivid image, that God is not to be thought of in his dealings with us as one who uses the canal, with its direct and confining channel, but rather the river which winds its way slowly and circuitously to the sea.

This is a pivotal point in our consideration of power, for we can hardly devise an appropriate strategy if we go one way while God operates in a manner quite different. What is clear, it seems to me, is that the "gracious relationship" of God to us is never a matter of irresistible might. Look for a moment at two areas in which God deals with us and note, in each case, how inappropriate it is to apply to his manner of working the figure of might or power.

The incarnation, central to Christian faith, is the record of one who "though he was in the form of God, did not count equality with God a thing to be grasped, but emptied himself, taking the form of a servant" (Philippians 2:6-7). Everything about the life of Jesus as portrayed in the Gospels increases our perplexity as to how he could have been endowed with the trappings of power. His birth was quiet, taking place in a stable, because his parents could command no better place. Joseph and Mary were of peasant stock, poor and undistinguished. His arrival was noted only by a few shepherds. Growing up in Nazareth, he made no great impact. Embarking on a public ministry, he called a group of ordinary men to be his disciples and with them went about teaching, preaching, and healing. Consistently throughout his ministry, he indicated that he had come to establish a new kingdom in which ordinary ways of accounting greatness would be inappropriate. When a dispute arose among the disciples as to the meaning of greatness, he took a little child, surely a symbol of powerlessness, and placed the child in their midst and said, "Whoever receives this child in my name receives me, and whoever receives me receives him who sent me; for he who is least among you all is the one who is great" (Luke 9:48). On another occasion, he urged that his followers repudiate the world's way of exercising lordship and "let the greatest among you become as the youngest, and the leader as one who serves" (Luke 22:26).

But the understanding of Jesus and his way is not dependent in the final sense on proof texts; it rests with the impact made by a fresh reading of the Gospels. There we confront one who finally expressed the ultimate insight of his being in his willingness to go to the cross, thereby making clear both the weakness of power (Pilate is remembered only in connection with Jesus) and the power of weakness, because the cross has been the illumination of God's way through the ages.

The incarnation is a vivid reminder to us that God did not seek to dazzle us into submission; he invited us to pilgrimage, in the course of which new levels of truth would be disclosed. The divine was present in Jesus but it was a reticent presence, necessitated by God's incredible concern for our integrity. Only God could have come in such hidden and yet such persuasive lowliness.

This contention is borne out also if we look at the church. Surely if God had intended to ride roughshod over us, giving us no chance to spurn him, he would have created an institution quite different from the church known in history. Not even in the New Testament period, despite our persistent tendency to glorify that time in unrealistic fashion, was the church anything approaching what it should have been. Always—then and now—it has been marked by apostasy and division, by acrimony and strife, by alliance with powers that cared nothing at all for the Christian cause. It has always been, and is at this time, an earthen vessel which has in its keeping the precious truth of God's message.

Once again, it can be affirmed that the divine is in the church. No matter how far the church departs from what it ought to be, it can never quite efface the reality of its divine nature. If it were not in some way a divine institution, brought into being and sustained by God for his own purpose, surely it would long since have ceased to exist. But the divine quality of its life is not such as to dazzle our minds into submission. It is only enough to elicit our commitment. For God always deals with us, not in terms of power and might, but in terms of grace and truth.

When we examine the way in which God actually deals with us, we recognize that terms such as might and power are singularly inappropriate. While God is not limited by anything external to himself, he does limit himself to enter into relationship with persons only in ways consistent with his nature as love. To start from any other basis, especially from a basis which exalts power to the highest point, is to imperil the Christian understanding of God's nature. It is also, as we have contended, to put the churches in a position of jeopardy in dealing with power.

Perspectives on Power

The foregoing reflections have not been an idle exercise. Such considerations, in which an attempt is made to understand the manner of God's working, are essential to the development of effective strategy. For no strategy for the churches in the eighties in regard to the manner of relating to power structures or anything else can have any hope of effectiveness if it is based on a theological foundation which lacks real authenticity. Such a foundation is to be found, not by listening to what the world says it wants, but by more disciplined reflection on who God is. To cease to regard power as an essential attribute of God is a necessary first step. We can be liberated by such understanding into a kind of relationship to power which will neither permit its avoidance in order to be pure nor its utilization without reservation in order to be dominant.

We need, in the light of this discussion, to consider aspects of relationship to power which characterize various agencies today. *The New Yorker* some time ago had an interesting reflection in its "The Talk of the Town" section about power. The reflections were prompted by a remark made by Benjamin Bradlee, executive editor of the Washington *Post*. He had been asked which paper, the *Post* or the *New York Times*, was the more powerful. The anonymous writer in *The New Yorker* said:

> In our opinion, power is the last thing that a newspaper should aim for. . . . Indeed, when reporters begin to interest themselves in power, and begin to consider themselves the equals of people who really are powerful . . . they are in danger of losing their effectiveness altogether. To our mind, it is endlessly instructive in the ways of journalism that the Watergate story was broken by two metropolitan-desk reporters, who had no experience in covering national politics, while scores of White House reporters, who were close to the seat of power, were somehow paralyzed.[9]

If close identification with power is dangerous for newspaper reporters, it is fatal to those whose vocation it is to keep power under constant scrutiny and assessment in the light of moral realities.

Observation in recent decades and reflection upon historical events lead to the formulation of an axiom: neither the academic nor the ecclesiastic should ever be too closely identified with the wielders of power. The reason is not that the wielding of power is so evil that it should not be attempted; it is, rather, that power and the aura surrounding those who have it make evaluation difficult. It is much too easy to be overwhelmed by the panoply of power and, as a result, to lose the ability to see through the impressive outward trappings to the realities underneath. Adolf A. Berle has pinpointed the way in which intellectuals are helpless before power—and ecclesiastics are surely no better at the task. He writes:

> Unhappily, the intellectuals are often plain pushovers for politicians and propagandists, in power or out. Within their fields of competence they have unlimited expertise in analyzing, studying, and solving problems, in exposing error and pretense, in forming opinion. . . . Their weakness lies in the fact that the issues on which they have and express opinions frequently lie outside their competence.[10]

A particularly clear example of this, as far as intellectuals are concerned, can be seen in the work of two fine political scientists and historians. James MacGregor Burns and Arthur M. Schlesinger, Jr., both wrote with distinction and discernment on the career of Franklin D. Roosevelt. Neither was directly involved in the day-to-day exercise of power by F.D.R. and this doubtless had much to do with the grasp of reality they both demonstrated in assessing his career. While both were genuinely affirmative about much done in the New Deal years, they nevertheless had a realistic appraisal of both political and personal weaknesses. When one turns, however, to their writing about John F. Kennedy, one is saddened by the lack of any real penetration. They were too closely associated with power, and consequently their judgments were distorted. They proved unable to arrive at any cogent summary of John F. Kennedy's personal qualities or his presidential performance. They therefore ended up able to do little more than contribute to a mystique, confusing surface glamor with significant accomplishment. It was, after all, Camelot; they were themselves part of it; and it was all lovely. Two such fine writers are especially melancholy examples because they serve as a warning that if this can happen with minds as sharp and disciplined as these, the prospects of what might happen with the less gifted are indeed frightening.

Ecclesiastics fare no better than academics. Two figures as different as Billy Graham and Reinhold Niebuhr illustrate the peril. Many have watched with sadness as Billy Graham, with immense prestige and with unparalleled access to the corridors of power and to the ear of the powerful, finally did little more than speak what power wanted to hear. It was invariably a word of support and reached its saddest point when, confronting the monumental abuses of power by Richard Nixon, he could only lament the earthy language of the tapes. "My message," he once said, "is so intensely personal that people miss the overwhelming social content."[11] It is probably just as well to leave that statement without critical evaluation; it reminds one of George Orwell's *1984* and the extinction of meaning. Confronting the moral enormity of Vietnam and then of Watergate, Billy Graham could do nothing other than utter supportive statements about what power was doing. No amount of specious distinction-making between the role of Old Testament prophet and New Testament evangelist can excuse moral blindness of that magnitude.

If this uncritical support was typical of Billy Graham, it must also be acknowledged that Reinhold Niebuhr's thought, despite its richness and helpfulness at so many points, runs into a similar danger of justifying power's actions. In Niebuhr's case, his thought finally differed very little from the hard-boiled formulations of United States policy arrived at with no regard for Christian insights at all. It is clear that Niebuhr himself retained a transcendent reference which prevented an easy capitulation to power, but in his polemical intensity he did not always deal with the "hardheaded" as devastatingly as he did with the "softhearted." Ernest Becker, commenting on Niebuhr's *Man's Nature and His Communities,* wrote in a letter: "Evidently Niebuhr's new book is a hard look at his own 'realism' with a view to a more idealistic stance. This is dynamite!—the one thing, as you know, that I always had against him." [12] While Niebuhr's position seems vastly better than Billy Graham's, so that there is hesitance in linking the two, I wish that he had spent as much time on the pitfalls of realism as he did on the illusions of idealism.

Too close an alliance with power not only distorts discernment, but it also displaces the Christian community from its proper place of identification. It is the task of the Christian community to stand with and for the oppressed and the poor. Not only is this the proper standing place for the churches, but it is also the only way in which the message of the Bible can be truly heard. Past identification with the wielders of power has left us with the task of recovering a standpoint which will enable us to hear the Bible again with real power. If this is to take place, we must heed the truth behind the words of Karl Barth: "God always takes His stand unconditionally and passionately on this side and on this side alone: against the lofty and on behalf of the lowly; against those who already enjoy right and privilege and on behalf of those who are denied it and deprived of it." [13] So clear is this in the Bible that one can express amazement that Christian churches have so often and so consistently abandoned that place and accepted with haste the proffered place with the powerful and the oppressive. The Christian churches, serving a Lord who came to seek and save the lost, fulfill the Lord's mandate only in a consistent and, if need be, costly commitment to the lowest elements of a given society. The churches must take seriously the passage from Isaiah used by Jesus in Luke 4. And no amount of cautious interpretation can take from the passage and countless others the most radical implications.

The identification of the churches with the holders of power involves the serious danger of a loss of insight into the nature of God's world. It is very easy, once that alliance has been firmly cemented, to move to a place where the panoply of worldly power suggests a structure utterly impregnable. How can churches, confronting such power, ever hope to change anything? From that question it is so very easy to move to the conclusion that worldly power actually represents a force against which nothing can avail. The simplest course then is to move to a place within that structure, operating on the principle that if you can't beat them, then join them. History is full of illustrations showing how this is done.

It is the thesis of Paul Lehmann, in his *The Transfiguration of Politics,* that such a reading of the situation is an act of unbelief. What distinguishes the believer, as we noted before, is a conviction that Jesus represented the power of weakness set over against the weakness of power. Such a position rests ultimately upon the foundation of a solid theology, which is developed out of the resources of the churches' own tradition and therefore refuses to determine its course by waiting to see how the winds of secularity are blowing.

The peril of power, as Lehmann to his credit recognizes, needs to be seen not only in the wielders of power but also in those who mount a revolution against established power. Christian thought, instructed in the realities of human nature, should have no place for romantic notions of the pristine purity of revolutionaries. "The bitter experience of the revolutionary," Lehmann writes, "is that established power never yields; hence it must be seized. The bitter experience of established power is that once established, it justifies itself as necessary and earned."[14] Some Christians today seem to be captured by the whimsical idea that revolutions, simply because their aims are noble, are miraculously delivered from the sins which beset establishments. Theological grounding helps us to realize, once again in the words of Paul Lehmann, that "All revolutions aspire to give human shape to the freedom that being and staying human take; and all revolutions end by devouring their own children."[15] The thorny issue of how much change society can experience, and how fast that change can be effected in and by society, will need to be looked at in the next chapter.

A Cautious Use of Power

What has thus far been written leaves Christians in an uncomfortable situation. The danger of power has been affirmed, and yet it has been insisted that Christians have no justification for renouncing it in a quest for purity. There is no way by which to deny the difficulty of our situation.

There are at least four possible approaches that can be taken in regard to power. (1) Some tender-minded versions of Christian faith simply deny the reality of power. (2) Other traditions dismiss power as totally evil and call upon Christians to refuse to wield it. (3) As we have seen in much of Christian history, the Christian communities have given power an unambiguous blessing. And (4) some Christian bodies recognize power as inevitable but also as dangerous.

It is this last strategy which holds promise. It must also be admitted, however, that it makes extremely difficult demands. What needs to be sought is an approach which will permit Christians personally and corporately to share in the wielding of power while at the same time retaining a lively conviction of its danger.

During the period of World War II, when earnest efforts were being made to place such events in a theological perspective, H. Richard Niebuhr wrote two articles for *The Christian Century*. In these articles, entitled "War as the Judgment of God" and "War as Crucifixion," he made an immensely helpful attempt to determine what such a tragic event meant in terms of faith. His endeavor was to center his attention, not on what the self or the enemy might be doing, but on what God was doing. He pointed out that "to attend to God's action is to be on the way to constructive understanding and constructive human reaction which the prophets initiated."[16] Out of his analysis emerged the insight that war involved the Christian themes of judgment and crucifixion.

To approach war from this type of vantage point had direct implications for the way in which Christians waged the struggle. What is required, Niebuhr affirmed, is

the abandonment of all self-defensiveness, all self-aggrandizement, all thinking in terms of the self as central. . . . It is to wage war as those do who will not withdraw when their own interests are no longer apparently imperiled while their weaker neighbors remain in danger, who will not wash their hands of the affair if the peace is not to their liking, but who, on the contrary, accept continuous, never ending responsibility for their neighbors.[17]

The call for the abandonment of self is only part of what is involved; for Niebuhr, taking the cross as the ultimate disclosure of God's way of dealing with evil, affirms that the Christian is called "to repentance, to a total revolution of our minds and hearts. And such a call to repentance—not to sorrow but to spiritual revolution—is an act of grace, a great recall from the road to death which we all travel together, the just and the unjust, the victors and the vanquished."[18]

There is, of course, no neat and complete parallel between the tragedy of global conflict and the wielding of power, and no such correspondence is claimed here. Yet power, while it does not kill, manifests itself in manipulation and sometimes in actual evil treatment of human beings. While war may kill the physical selves of the enemies, power often does evil to the spiritual selves of those over whom it is exercised. Hence the parallel, while far from neat, is not without its illumination.

It is manifestly a very difficult task to which Christians are summoned. The mixed nature of power, in which it can neither be renounced without question nor exercised without caution, makes it incredibly complex. Yet it seems that Christians who will take seriously the symbols of faith will find that power can be approached with something of the same spirit as that in which H. Richard Niebuhr sought to make sense of World War II. Involved in this would be the willingness to wield power, just as there was willingness to wage war; responsibility was a Christian call in each instance. At the same time, there would be a recognition that both war and power are dangerous and can be entered into only if there is a resolute deliverance from self and a liberation into love for neighbor. Moreover, the waging of war and the wielding of power need to be infused with a constant sense of repentance. For the pathos of power, in our modern societies, is that even if the person wielding it is good and decent, one can nevertheless never be exempt from doing evil. The structures of modern society are such that evil is endemic in the exercise of power. This is a fact which Christian faith may help us to see with clarity. When this is clearly understood, the evil effects of power are kept within limits. When the powerful know they are sinful, they can be kept open to the springs of love and compassion. It is the powerful who imagine themselves virtuous who create havoc. By its steadfast reminder that all are sinners, Christian faith can put wholesome restraints on the exercise of power.

5

The Radical Middle

A *New Yorker* cartoon of the late sixties caught with considerable accuracy a widespread mood. The cartoonist depicted an Establishment-type father with his hand on the shoulder of his anti-Establishment, bearded son. The caption read: "Look, Son, I'm a far-right conservative and you're a far-left radical. O. K.? So lets you and me go out and beat up some liberals." To "beat up some liberals" became a popular pastime. After the onslaught somewhat subsided, the surviving liberalism was a tattered and bedraggled point of view. Its adherents were—and, to some degree, still are—dispirited and uncertain. A new strategy is being sought.

The Heritage of Liberalism

Mention was made, in assessing the factors which created the problems of the sixties and seventies, of the tension existing between two traditions in Christian social theory. One tradition is that of social gospel liberalism, represented by Walter Rauschenbusch, and the other is Christian realism, represented by Reinhold Niebuhr. At that point, the intention was simply to make clear the reality of the tension. (See pages 28-33.) Now our task is to endeavor to resolve the tension and to see whether in our new setting there are usable

81

elements in both social gospel liberalism and in Christian realism.

This particular time, when we are preparing for mission in the eighties, is a propitious one in which to attempt such a reassessment. Enough distance now separates us from social gospel liberalism to see it in perspective. The same thing is true, to a somewhat lesser degree, of Christian realism. No longer involved in the pyrotechnics of controversy, we are delivered from partisanship which produced polemics. Perhaps we are now advantageously situated to attempt formulation of an outlook which will unashamedly borrow what is usable in both traditions, and we may be liberated in the process from caring whether the resulting new approach fully resembles either of the previous outlooks.

What this venture will make clear is the fact that much of our work in Christian social theory consists in rummaging in theological attics for discarded items. When found and brought out to the light, they are often discovered to be usable, if not in their present form, then slightly modified. In other words, we are often involved, not in introducing a startling innovation, but in refurbishing a strategic rediscovery. Such a process is a necessary part of preparing for Christian social action in the eighties.

The social gospel came to us closely allied with theological liberalism. Most of the formative figures in the development of the social gospel were also liberal in social politics. The two went hand-in-hand. The situation was quite otherwise in the development of Christian realism. As might be expected, in a movement which delighted in paradox, realism found its devotees emphasizing truths in older doctrines, original sin for example, while at the same time being committed to a radical social posture. A collision was inevitable, and the dust of the conflict has only recently begun to settle.

Clearly, liberalism has been under relentless examination and attack for the past few decades. As a result, anybody still desiring to bear the label and do the work of liberalism is bound to feel a measure of discomfort. This may be part of the familiar "failure of nerve" syndrome of which so much has been made. If the attacks have not always carried conviction, forcing the abandonment of the liberal stance, they have had the effect of depriving liberals of much joy in their outlook.

What has happened is that liberalism, once a passionate faith, sank into the platitudinous. It achieved too soon so many of its goals that its adherents and its antagonists alike concluded that it had finished its essential work. Failing to develop new goals, it succumbed to a dangerous illusion: it assumed that it had arrived. Once that point had been reached, liberalism saw its essential role as that of defending what had been achieved and lost sight of the important truth that the genius of liberalism, the one quality without which it becomes drab and unexciting, must always include, along with the defense of what is good in a heritage, a constant development of new and exciting agendas. While liberalism can often endure the attacks of its critics, it can never survive the complacency of its adherents.

The liberal debacle involves something more. Once the liberal was in the vanguard, self-consciously proud of that fact, aware of being honorably different. The liberal has found it hard indeed to adjust to the fact of being merely part of an amorphous middle. So much had been achieved that liberalism knew the failure of success. The liberal triumph had become the liberal defeat.

Whatever else might be said about it, the middle is not a place of either enchantment or excitement. Admitting the validity in much of the critique of liberalism, a question remains: if liberalism is indeed without enchantment or excitement, is it possible that it compensates by continuing to nourish a more fundamental virtue? Is it, in short, possible that the liberal position embodies the stance of the responsible person? Modern liberalism, which has been closely aligned with the middle classes, has created a middle which is not comfortable to occupy. That particular terrain has been called by a variety of terms—"the vital center" (Arthur M. Schlesinger, Jr.), "the radical middle" (Renata Adler). Perhaps, however, the most accurate designation is that of the literary critic, George Steiner, who called it "the impossible middle." In reviewing the collected essays, journalism, and letters of George Orwell, Steiner pointed out that the essayist and novelist came to his basic position during his time of service in the Spanish Civil War. "It was there," Steiner said, "that he chose the impossible middle, equidistant from the lies and raptures of totalitarianism, be it of the right or of the left."[1] This "impossible middle" has become, however, more attractive recently than it has been in the past. Any effective strategy for Christian social action in the eighties must incorporate elements of social gospel liberalism.

Reason and Hope

What, then, is usable in social gospel liberalism? Bearing in mind that our enterprise is one of finding discarded but important items in the theological attic, it is time for us to assert again the indispensable role to be played in both theological formulation and social policy determination by reason.

No one, looking back at the sixties, can be other than impressed by the rejection of reason characteristic of the period. It was as though an intolerable restraint had been lifted and many rushed fervently into the new arena, where the "pale cast of thought" no longer inhibited robust—and frequently violent—action. Impressed by the degree to which reason was tied up with the prevailing culture, the partisans of the adversary culture wanted nothing to do with it. They rejected anything that smacked of the rational and threw themselves with ardor and abandon into states of consciousness, sometimes drug-induced, sometimes not, but which in any event owed nothing to reason, and into forms of social action which erupted spontaneously and were divorced as far as possible from any rationally articulated premises or programs. Animated by the blissful, irrational idea that *anything* which replaced the current system had to be an improvement, there was no attempt to calculate what might be the consequences of any course of action, whether it was violence against the citadel of prejudice in the South or North or against the obvious enemies of the new who sat safely ensconced in the administration buildings of universities. It was the action itself which, by some mysterious magic, would make *their* deeds, no matter how violent, beneficent in their ultimate results.

To criticize such mindlessness is by no means a defense of what a supposedly rational society has permitted to take place. The flaw in the argument which claims that our society, up to the period of irrationality on the part of activists in the sixties, had been one which countenanced vicious oppressions and the inexpressible evil of the Holocaust and that therefore reason is to be repudiated lies in the admission that such a society was neither reasonable nor rational. It was most assuredly not reasonable; and a sharp distinction needs to be maintained between the potential values of reason and what some of its supposed practitioners permit in its name. A society of war and genocide is not reasonable; it is the antithesis of the reasonable. We should be able to penetrate behind the smoke screen and see that, no matter how insistently a society may have tried to label itself reasonable, it was nothing of the kind.

Furthermore, to call for reason's employment in both religion and social action is not to fall victim to the idea that reason is all-sufficient. Of course, it is not; and the emphases now being heard as corrections of one-sided rationalism are welcome indeed. To state that reason has limits is to state the obvious. But to go on and argue that since reason has limits it must be abandoned is surely a type of folly. What needs to be done is to let reason carry the enterprise, whether of thought or of action, as far as possible. Having reached that place, you must then wager with Pascal or leap with Kierkegaard or risk action on behalf of a cause. No point, however, is served in forcing the wager to be astronomically high or the leap impossibly wide. But action must at some point be undertaken, and that point will always be reached without all the relevant facts one would like to possess and without the clear perception of consequences one would like to have. Surely, no one would deny these marks of all human existence.

The matter was put well by Santayana some time ago:

> Finding their intelligence enslaved, our contemporaries supposed that intelligence is essentially servile; instead of freeing it, they try to elude it. Not free enough themselves morally . . . they cannot think of rising to a detached contemplation of earthly things, and of life itself and evolution; they revert rather to sensibility, and seek some by-path of instinct or dramatic sympathy in which to wander. Having no stomach for the ultimate, they burrow themselves downwards towards the primitive.[2]

Burrowing down to the primitive is hardly the way to move toward civilization.

If Christian mission in the eighties is in need of social gospel liberalism's reliance upon reason, it is also in need of the hopefulness which characterized the social gospel. We must be careful at this point, since this is one of the ticklish areas where Christian realism and social gospel liberalism came into sharp conflict. Liberalism, at a particular historical juncture, needed the trenchant criticism of realism at the point of liberalism's extravagant hopes; we shall return to this matter in our discussion of the usable elements in realism. But right now it is necessary to stress the reality of disenchantment and frustration. The current mood is far removed from the expansive hopefulness of an earlier day, and it is with this mood fully in mind that we must assess the new needs.

It requires no elaboration of examples or incidents to clinch the argument that modern people are troubled. What Reinhold Niebuhr called "the easy conscience of modern man," has, thanks in part to his thought and in larger part to historical buffeting, pretty much passed from the scene. Supposed innocence has fled before realities like Vietnam and Watergate and continuing revelations of ethical impropriety. The modern person, as a result of these and other social calamities, is caught in a paralyzing hopelessness. The temptation to sin faced today is perhaps not so much the pride for which Niebuhr chastised us in the recent past as the apathy which Harvey Cox condemns on the contemporary scene.

There is no possibility—and certainly no desire here to suggest—that we go back to the hopefulness characteristic of social gospel liberalism. That phase is over. But Christian mission in the eighties, if it is to head for open seas, must by some means find a way by which to kindle new hopefulness.

It has already been admitted that the expectations of social gospel liberalism were extravagant and unreal. They served badly, because they infused many with hopes that experience was bound to disappoint. The somber word of Christian realism about the folly of utopian expectations was a needed corrective. It is now apparent that realism, in its turn, needs the corrective of social gospel emphasis on the possibility of change. The phrasing is careful and deliberate: it is not any guarantee of progress which is needed, but only the affirmation of history as an arena of possibilities.

It is significant to note that failure to nourish a sense of possibility was one of the criticisms directed against Christian realism. Participating in a symposium on Christian realism under the auspices of *Christianity and Crisis*, Harvey Cox leveled at realism the criticism that it failed to sound a sufficiently strong note of hope and possibility. He said:

> A future historian of Christian ethics might suggest that Niebuhr was responsible for and should be thanked for the reintroduction into

American thought of Augustinian-Reformation realism about society and man's possibilities in society. . . .

I would suggest, however, that in addition to the Augustinian tradition in Christianity there is also what Benz calls the Joachimite tradition. This is the visionary or sectarian tradition. I have some roots in this tradition, and I think it is an equally reputable one. . . . I would hope that what is happening now is the restoration of a kind of balance, or we might say a dialectic, between these two traditions.

We can't go back to being abolitionists or suffragettes, or even Walter Rauschenbusch social gospelers. We have been scourged and corrected by history and by theological reflection since then. But I think there is something very valuable in that tradition which nonetheless can form political action in the future.[3]

This is the sort of thing which social gospel liberalism stressed—the possibility of real and significant changes in the social order.

Vitally important, of course, in the development of strategies is a sense of timing. In an era of expansive optimism there was clearly a need for astringent and harsh dealing with superficialities. But in an era when human hopes are fragile indeed and the sense of possibility has eroded in serious fashion, there is something rather callous in doing nothing more than pronouncing a benediction over decadent civilizations. It should be kept in mind that many younger persons never knew optimism as the social gospel affirmed it. They are sons and daughters of disenchantment and that fact needs to be kept clearly in mind. They do not need so much to be humbled—events have done that—as to be encouraged and nurtured in hope.

Even within Christian realism—and especially in the thought of Reinhold Niebuhr himself—there are affirmations of the real possibilities of human history. Because he was so concerned with demolishing the illusions of liberalism, Niebuhr did not go out of his way to affirm such possibilities. The puncturing of illusion is far more prevalent than the affirmation of possibility. But the affirmations are there, and his outlook was so rooted in the sense of God's living reality in human history that he could never set arbitrary limits. His Gifford Lectures include this ringing affirmation of human hope:

He is also anxious because he does not know the limits of his possibilities. He can do nothing and regard it perfectly done, because higher possibilities are revealed in each achievement. All human actions stand under seemingly limitless possibilities. There are, of course, limits but it is difficult to gauge them from any immediate perspective.[4]

This sense of ever new possibilities is what is needed in our era.

It is clearly a far cry from that kind of possibility to any guarantee of progress. It is, indeed, possible to be quite pessimistic about probabilities, reasonably sure, given human nature as it is, that there are going to be very dismaying consequences to any course of action. That is not the crucial matter. Along with the pessimism about probabilities there needs to go a firm affirmation of possibilities. The human spirit, especially when upheld by a firm Christian faith which rests both human origin and human destiny in God, needs no easy assurances; it does require vital possibilities. Such a sense of possibility was one of the significant legacies of social gospel liberalism, and at this time, purged of its aberrations and exaggerations, it can help in preparing Christians for responsible social action in the eighties.

The Contribution of Realism

A peril of any movement toward social reform is that it must kindle high hopes. Such hopes are the motive force essential to nerve persons to join in a cause in which sacrifice and suffering may be experienced. It is the glowing hope that first enlists persons in the cause and it is the hope which often keeps them from despair. No matter how admirable Albert Camus may find the figure of Sisyphus, forever rolling that stone to the top of the hill and forever having it roll right back to the bottom, it is not likely that Sisyphus will be adopted as the patron saint of social activists. In order to sustain social action over a long period of time, it is not essential to believe that the stone will either remain at the top of the hill or even finally make it to that point. Social action can be sustained if it rolls back down the hill again, but it is dubious whether you can sustain the commitment if you never can start from any point higher than the previous time. Some real movement upward, if only modest, is enough to sustain effort. It seems clear, however, that such modest encouragement is needed.

Social gospel liberalism, we have said, was not wrong in affirming some real degree of possibility of change in human affairs. What happened was unfortunate, because the hopes engendered lost all contact with historical possibility. The hopes necessary to sustain effort and sacrifice became so extravagant as to be impossible, and we thus confront the melancholy sight of despair produced by failure to achieve the hopes which originally inspired effort. Social hopes became transformed into Utopian expectations. What had been a spur to effort became a fertile source of illusion.

It was the consistent intention of Reinhold Niebuhr and the movement of Christian realism to dispel the illusion of perfectibility. Convinced that this illusion was the breeding ground for much of religion's social ineffectiveness, realism hammered away at the task of demolishing the flimsy structures of social gospel liberalism. A complex picture was presented by realism. To expect the kingdom of God to come within the bounds of human history was folly. All growth toward order in society was accompanied by possibilities of chaos. Against this chaos order had to struggle continually, and there was no cogent ground for assuming that order would ever achieve the victory. Since love was defined in such radical terms as unconcern for self, it was not of any use in the relations between social groups. In no way could such groups ascend to the pinnacle of abandonment of all concern for self-interest. Hence love, as an instrument of guidance in social policy, was out of place. It was too tender for the tough world of politics. The choices confronting the Christian in society are never neat and perfect. Because this was the abiding situation of the Christian in social struggles, Christian faith could never serve effectively as an instrument of guidance. Realism saw faith as a solace in defeat, a source of forgiveness for inevitable sin, and an instrument of judgment to guard against premature complacency. Faith was thus relegated, as far as Christian realism was concerned, to a place of importance after action had been taken; it had little role to play in determining policy in advance of its implementation. Niebuhr wrote:

> We never have the chance to choose between pure tyranny and pure freedom; we can only choose between tyranny and relative democracy. We do not have the choice between war and perfect peace, but only between war and the uneasy peace of some fairly decent and stable equilibrium of social forces. We cannot choose between violence and non-violence, but only between violence and a statesmanship which seeks to adjust social forces without violence but cannot guarantee immunity from clashes. We have never had the opportunity—and probably never shall have—to choose between injustice and perfect equality, but only between injustice and a justice which moves toward equality and incorporates some of its values.[5]

Though those words come from one of his earlier books, they state an approach to social policy which did not change over the years.

Realism built upon this basic insight and contended that not only are our choices at this moment always less than perfect but also such a condition is a permanent aspect of human existence. No day would ever come when the Christian acting in politics would be granted neat and pure choices. The social order which resulted from all the less-than-perfect choices would continue indefinitely to be less than ideal. The sentimental notion that the ethic of Jesus, if only it were taken seriously, would lead humanity into the kingdom of God on earth was to Christian realism wildly visionary and the source of dangerous illusions.

The weakness of social gospel liberalism was its alliance with a culture which was confident of humanity's ability to achieve perfection within history. It was history itself which was redemptive. The eschatological element in the biblical tradition was an embarrassment to the adherents of historical hope. While history had in it a teleological element, so that it headed toward a destined fulfillment, it had no eschatological element calling for a final conflict between the forces of Christ and anti-Christ. Despite some emphasis in Rauschenbusch which bowed in the direction of the classical Christian understanding and despite his development of the concept of the Kingdom of Evil, it can hardly be denied that he trusted too complacently in social processes to bear humanity toward a this-worldly goal of a perfect society.

Christian realism saw no grounds for such hope. Robert E. Fitch has pointed out that Reinhold Niebuhr's view of history includes three basic affirmations, each of which is in opposition to social gospel liberalism. First, history has "unity by faith but not by sight." It progresses toward both chaos and cosmos. Second, it "affirms the ultimate character of sin and of evil in history." Because of this, history can never be redemptive; it cannot be, says Fitch, "its own Christ." Third, "history provides a disclosure of meaning but not a fulfillment of meaning."[6] We are always, in a figure Niebuhr used, like Moses who glimpsed the Promised Land from afar and who had made some progress toward it but would never enter it in history.

It is hardly surprising that this onslaught of realism was bitterly resisted in American social gospel circles. It hit with a shock, calling into question many of the assumed simplicities which had become the staples of the outlook of social gospel liberalism. Such a view, offered as realism, was dismissed as pessimism, and it was contended that the pure atmosphere of American theological and social thought was being contaminated by the importation of despairing views from European disenchantment. But when the polemics are over and a sober estimate is attempted, it is clear that Christian social theory was badly in need of this somber realism.

It was a realism needed in order to keep vision clear. As long as Christian social action is predicated on the possibility of perfection, social realities are not seen clearly. In his own career, in the articles which poured from his fertile mind and engaged spirit, Niebuhr tore the veneer from the respectable social order and exposed the realities hidden underneath. He thereby restored to Christian social action a sense of reality which had been lacking. Once it is acknowledged that no arrangement is going to be perfect, one is far more likely to look with discernment at what is going on. Unlike Rauschenbusch, affirming that the family, education, and politics had all been Christianized, one lives with the constant understanding that *no* earthly arrangement will ever be perfect. One is accordingly ready to see what is wrong.

Moreover, this realism preserves a transcendent source of judgment. The domestication of Christian faith, a process by which the easy identification of Christian faith and modern culture takes place, is avoided by realism's stern reminder that no perfection is ever found. "Only in a religion in which there is a true sense of transcendence can we find the resource to convict every historical achievement of incompleteness, and to prevent the sanctification of the relative values of any age or any era."[7] Christian realism's insistence on this point is a significant service to Christian social action.

Back of the repudiation of perfectionist illusion is realism's recovery of the fact of sin. It was this rediscovery which produced the sober analysis of historical possibility. It is likely that the restatement of the doctrine of sin and the profound analysis of the meaning of sin as pride will remain one of the most significant contributions of realism to Christian living in our day.

A serious flaw of liberalism was that it failed to see this reality with clarity. It was much too inclined to accept humanity at its own high estimate. Any emphasis on the reality of sin was looked upon as somehow degrading and a denial of the bright possibilities of human life. Most of the time in liberalism there was an assumption that what was wrong with human beings was not a radical defect but a minor dysfunction. The trouble may have been in an animal inheritance not yet outgrown or a lack of knowledge or a failure to try seriously the way of Jesus. The remedy for the defect, however, was considered always to be within the person's potential. A bit more effort, additional knowledge, a firmer commitment—these would assuredly overcome the defect.

Such superficial thinking was exposed by realism's more profound analysis, an analysis which illumined what was actually taking place far better than liberalism's blissful and naive confidence in natural goodness. To liberalism's serene assurance realism brought the direct word of Alexander Miller that "the human dilemma will need for its resolution not a resolve but a rescue."[8]

The point at which this bears upon our concern is to note that the interpretation of human nature is not limited in its application. If the realist doctrine of sin is to be truly useful, it is required that it be applied to all persons. This means that it is characteristic of the holders of power and also characteristic of those who seek to overthrow the present occupants of the seats of the mighty. Our trouble often emerges because we fail to make this across-the-board application. At times we exempt the holders of power, and we operate on the strange assumption that the attainment of power must always bring with it the achievement of virtue. Realism helpfully explodes that myth. But no less does the analysis apply to the instruments of violent revolution. The whimsical idea that a noble cause enlists only noble people is no more tenable than the myth of the goodness of the powerful. In endeavoring to learn the lesson of the sixties, we need to take this seriously. The sixties were especially prone to the illusion that the opponents of the power structure had to be virtuous. Nat Hentoff once asked a radical of the sixties whether the new order would have any place for due process of law and was told, "There are times when those of us preparing a revolutionary society must simply go ahead and do what's right because we understand what's right better than anyone else." And Hentoff comments: "I saw the utter conviction with which he spoke and knew how sincere a jailer he could be."[9] It may seem a small service to remind partisans of a good cause that they are also subject to the sinfulness which infects all human actions, but it may finally prove to be the one insight which can keep social change from being simply a means by which one set of oppressors takes the place of another. It should serve also to caution against unrestrained utilization of violence, terrorism, and revolution. While the possibility that violence and revolution may be necessary cannot be automatically ruled out, since the existing regime may well be so profoundly evil that no other recourse is available, the application of Christian realism may moderate the fury of all sides and thus preserve a fragile sense of common humanity.

There is, admittedly, a kind of pick-and-choose procedure at work here. The resulting outlook has resemblances both to social gospel liberalism and to Christian realism. The product may seem to be a matter of patches here and there and may lack any real beauty. This is not the crucial matter. If such an outlook can preserve our hope and guide us by reason, and if we can avoid the illusion of utopian perfectionism by seeing clearly the reality of sin and evil, the radical middle may be the foundation for significant service in the eighties.

There is a question which needs to be faced. The outlook sketched here, developed out of the writings and witness of Walter Rauschenbusch and Reinhold Niebuhr, may come across fairly well within the covers of a book. But is it an outlook which can be of genuine help to Christians involved in social struggle? What we need now to do is to see what this approach would suggest in terms of the crucial social struggle of the recent past—the civil rights struggle in this country. We turn, then, to the task of taking a look at that struggle, keeping in mind the elements of the approach developed in these pages.

6

Tried in a Crucible

Each age of Christian mission has a unique character. In considering Christian mission in the eighties, it is obvious that we cannot discern its demands with complete confidence. An element of newness and surprise will be present. For the future is always clouded and God makes "all things new," thereby frustrating our efforts to be too secure in our assumptions. While this has to be taken into account, and while the admission should guard us against unwarranted rigidity, it nevertheless seems sure that the eighties will be similar enough to previous times to permit some utilization of forms of thought and social strategies which served in the past. So we seek to use the past in a creative way, utilizing the past without venerating it.

The future does not permit a simple continuation of past policies, taken unchanged into the present or future. While social gospel liberalism rendered a valuable service in its day, it cannot guide us effectively in the decade of the eighties. It is the same with Christian realism. Like social gospel liberalism, Christian realism rendered a real service to a particular age; but it is not adequate by itself for the future. Accordingly, Christian mission in the eighties needs the unhesitating, unapologetic commitment to social action which is a common bond of both social gospel liberalism and Christian realism. Along with this common concern, a tenable Christian approach to social action in the next decade needs the emphasis in social gospel liberalism on the need to utilize reason as a guide in the formulation of theology and in the determination of social strategies. Also needed is the conviction, purged of exaggerations, that change is possible in society as a result of hard and disciplined effort. From Christian realism we take its awareness of limits; utopian hopes represent luxuries we cannot afford. Also borrowed from Christian realism is its insight into the reality of sin and evil in society. These elements from the past, suitably refined in the light of fresh insights, remain valid and are essential for the development of an effective social strategy. Equipped with a set of convictions forged out of such elements, we can move ahead in the eighties with hope of faithfulness in our Christian mission. We know, of course, that changes and adaptations will be required along the way, and that all policies or theories we evolve are to be regarded as provisional and experimental. What we seek and need is an outlook firm enough to guide us but not so firm as to imprison us.

It is of some help to set out the elements needed in this theoretical fashion. Perhaps the effort may carry a degree of persuasion. But what would be more effective would be to discover that this outlook, far from being simply theoretical, has been embodied in the life and witness of an individual and utilized in a social movement.

Martin Luther King, Jr.

We do have the example of a specific human being whose action, worked out in the crucible of an epic struggle for human rights, blended creatively the elements already outlined. The social struggle was the movement for civil rights for black people in the United States. By looking at the life of one person and at the strategies for a social movement, we can discern the dynamics of a Christian social strategy for the eighties.

The person is, of course, Martin Luther King, Jr. In an age which has not produced much in the way of authentic greatness, he stands out vividly. It is unnecessary to canonize Martin Luther King; the attempt to do so would be a disservice to his memory. At the same time, it is appropriate to give thanks that God raised up the man for the moment and joined the person and the social need, as God has so often done, in fruitful relationship. A great cause, long approaching in the United States, found in a young black preacher one whose background, temperament, training, and inner spiritual strength uniquely fitted him to lead a movement for the ultimate emancipation of black and white people. There is greatness enough here without any unrealistic canonization of the man.

Similarly, the civil rights movement needs to be appraised with a determination to assess what was valid in it and a willingness to say what was invalid. It is folly to claim that this social movement was always wise in the strategies employed; no social movement has ever been able to claim soundness in all it did. It is, indeed, clear by this time that the civil rights movement was effective and creative in its early days, when it was guided by King's presence and directed by his vision of nonviolent pressure, and that it fell apart later on, after King's life was snuffed out by the assassin's bullet and the movement itself split into contending factions in which the steadfast emphasis on love was abandoned. The lessons, both positive and negative, of that period need to be pondered as Christians consider a form of social action appropriate for the eighties.

The importance of Martin Luther King, Jr., centers in the way he so creatively fused the elements which have been set forth as providing a foundation for social action in the eighties. It seems, looking at the time in retrospect, that every element in his background prepared him uniquely to fill the role which was finally his.

Martin Luther King, Jr., was fortunate in his rootage in a vibrant religious tradition. He was born in the South in a middle-class family. His father was a distinguished preacher and leader in the black community. The young Martin Luther King consequently absorbed in home and church the warm, strong Christian tradition which had sustained black people through vicissitudes which would otherwise have crushed them. Thanks to this background, his religion was a matter of feeling; intellectual rigor and sharpness would come later.

This vital Christian faith was no escapist outlook. The future leader of the black struggle saw early in his life the viciousness of racial bigotry and hatred. Speaking about his early teens in Atlanta, he said he had grown up abhorring not only segregation but also the oppressive and barbarous acts that grew out of it. I had passed spots where Negroes had been savagely lynched, and had watched the Ku Klux Klan on its rides at night. I had seen police brutality with my own eyes, and watched Negroes receive the most tragic injustice in the courts.[1]

It is clear that those early exposures to the oppression of black people remained to serve as incentives to costly effort and struggle in later years.

Against his father's wishes, Martin and his brother took jobs in a factory which employed both blacks and whites. His father had opposed this, because he did not want his sons to be subjected to oppressive conditions. The experience, however, provided the young Martin with a sense of economic injustice to go with his keen sense of racial injustice. His teen years, then, left him with a sense of a society which was shot through with injustice. What he had to seek was some means by which to attack such blatant evils. His subsequent training is a matter of seeing one essential ingredient being added after another, until the moment found the man fully prepared.

He acquired an important ingredient during his undergraduate days at Morehouse College. There he read Thoreau's *Essay on Civil Disobedience* for the first time. "Fascinated by the idea of refusing to cooperate with an evil system, I was so deeply moved that I reread the work several times. This was my first intellectual contact with the theory of nonviolent resistance."[2]

From Morehouse College, Martin Luther King, Jr., went to Crozer Theological Seminary in Chester, Pennsylvania. The atmosphere at Crozer was strongly on the liberal side in its interpretation of Christian faith. The liberalism which characterized the young Martin Luther King and was a constant element in his outlook throughout his life was never an uncritical one. As we shall see, he had to modify certain emphases after reading Reinhold Niebuhr, but this in no way alters the fact that his understanding of the meaning of Christian faith was consistently liberal.

So theological liberalism was added to the fervent religious faith and the vivid sense of injustice and oppression. The next encounter in his days of theological preparation was decisive. This was the impact made upon him by Walter Rauschenbusch and the social gospel. It is apparent that he was ready for this; he knew change was needed in the social order and what he sought was some framework which would make theologically valid this passion for social change. In his words he was embarked upon "a serious intellectual quest for a method to eliminate social evil." That quest brought him

> early to Walter Rauschenbusch's *Christianity and the Social Crisis,* which left an indelible imprint on my thinking by giving me a theological basis for the social concern which had already grown up in me as a result of my early experiences. . . . It has been my conviction ever since reading Rauschenbusch that any religion which professes to be concerned about the souls of men and is not concerned about the social and economic conditions that scar the soul is a spiritually moribund religion only waiting for the day to be buried.[3]

From Rauschenbusch, then, King took theological validation for social concern.

But what he calls his "pilgrimage to nonviolence" did not end with Walter Rauschenbusch. It is instructive, in the light of the contentions of the previous chapter, to note that he added an element from Reinhold Niebuhr to his outlook before he launched on his work. In common with many others, King found Niebuhr's thought a devastating blow to his earlier outlook. The encounter with Niebuhr "burst like a bombshell into King's liberal theological-ethical world view."[4] No more with Niebuhr than with Rauschenbusch was King guilty of an uncritical endorsement; there were elements in Niebuhr's viewpoint, especially his radically perfectionist definition of love, with which King was in disagreement. But this in no way lessens the importance of Niebuhr and Christian realism in the final achievement of King's mature outlook.

Moral Man and Immoral Society was the book by Niebuhr which made a significant impact on King. In that book, published in 1932, Niebuhr subjected liberalism to searching analysis and scathing attack. While King believed that Niebuhr interpreted nonviolence too much in passive terms, he accepted Niebuhrian insights at pivotal points. The naive optimism which had characterized theological liberalism was rejected by King in the light of the more penetrating analysis of human nature offered by Reinhold Niebuhr. Furthermore, King found great cogency in Niebuhr's insight into the way in which the wielders of power in society cling to that power, resisting all efforts to take it away. Hence no movement for social change can depend on moral suasion alone; it is power set against power which brings about change. One can see in this insight a truth utilized in Montgomery, Selma, and wherever King went.

In the existing situation only nonviolence offered any chance of success. The technique of nonviolence, Niebuhr said,

> will, if persisted in with the same patience and discipline attained by Mr. Gandhi and his followers, achieve a degree of justice which neither pure moral suasion nor violence could gain. . . . One waits for such a campaign with all the more reason and hope because the peculiar spiritual gifts of the Negro endow him with the capacity to conduct it successfully. He would need only to fuse the aggressiveness of the new and young Negro with the patience and forebearance of the old Negro, to rob the former of its vindictiveness and the latter of its lethargy.[5]

One wonders whether that remarkable passage was pondered and cherished by the young Martin Luther King.

It is interesting to see that Niebuhr himself felt that King had arrived at a strategy which gave promise of significant success. Niebuhr is quoted as saying that "Martin Luther King's position is right." He called him "the most creative Protestant, white or black."[6] In a letter to Ira Zepp, Niebuhr said:

> . . . my enthusiasm for Dr. King's nonviolence despite my anti-pacifism was due to my distinction between a pacifism designed to prove our purity and a pacifism designed to establish justice. I thought that Dr. King leading a ten percent Negro minority was a good combination of idealism and pragmatic realism[7]

—a judgment foreshadowed in the 1932 passage in *Moral Man and Immoral Society*.

These, then, were the elements with which Martin Luther King, Jr., armed with a Ph.D. from Boston University, returned to the South. It was in Montgomery, as pastor of the Dexter Avenue Baptist Church, that the preparations of mind and spirit were amply justified. When the epic struggle began with the arrest of Rosa Parks on December 1, 1955, the young pastor assumed his crucial role. "The Day of Days, December 5," arrived and the bus boycott began. The young minister became the leader of one of the most creative social movements in American history. He was ready. And so was the movement of the black people in response to his leadership. From December 5, 1955, to April 4, 1968, when the assassin's bullet ended his life, Martin

Luther King, Jr., led a movement which changed attitudes, altered structures, and brought new hope and dignity to black people everywhere.

Achievements in the Civil Rights Movement

On a gray February day in 1974 a young reporter looked out the window of the Atlanta *Constitution*'s pressroom in the Georgia capital. The drizzle poured down on the statue of Tom Watson. Howell Raines, the young reporter, recalled the dream Watson had of creating a Southern politics without racial hatred. On that day, Howell Raines realized that "the fulfillment of Tom Watson's dream was at hand. For a Southerner who had spent most of the previous decade as a reporter in Alabama and Georgia, the signs were too clear to be mistaken or ignored."[8]

Those signs were indeed impressive. Howell Raines recalled a day when George Wallace crowned a black woman as the University of Alabama's homecoming queen. He had seen Governor Jimmy Carter hang a portrait of Martin Luther King, Jr., in the rotunda of Georgia's capitol as one of the state's great citizens. These were impressive indications of a significant change which had taken place. But back of these events there was a story of an elemental struggle for human dignity, and on that day Howell Raines decided he would try to tell "a story that had not received the telling it deserved. And this story, I was convinced, would be best told by the people who had lived it."[9] Armed with this insight and with a tape recorder, he set out to get that story down. The result, told in his book *My Soul Is Rested*, is a thrilling one indeed.

As one person after another tells his or her story, a sense of the significance of the struggle emerges. Ordinary people, with no chance to polish what they are saying, rise to genuine eloquence as they speak about the movement. Howell Raines himself affirms that the eloquence of the account is due to something more than the genius of all Southerners for telling stories marvelously well. A deeper quality was at work in what they did, and that deeper quality is reflected in their manner of recounting what it was like to be involved. It is, he says, the "mysterious eloquence in people who have lived with greatness."[10]

In light of the earlier discussion in which we suggested that a valid

Christian social strategy for the eighties needs the emphasis of social gospel liberalism on the possibility of significant social change, the civil rights movement provides ample documentation of the soundness of this principle. Not only did change take place but also those who brought it about were animated by a conviction of precisely such a possibility. This confidence was born, not simply of a study of social movements and the consequent development of a strategy, but out of the soil of deep and fervent religious conviction. It must never be forgotten that the civil rights movement emerged out of the churches and found a major part of its leadership in the pastors of those churches. A theological foundation lay beneath all such efforts, and it included a vivid sense of a God of love and justice who was himself deeply involved in the struggles of oppressed people.

If any social movement is to make a real impact, it has to have some idea of how God is related to the structures of society. Paul Lehmann has argued that the "critical question" is whether God is upholding the world by changing it, or changing the world by upholding it. He says:

> If God is doing the second, then the given patterns and structures are the fundamental supports indispensable to having any world at all; then order has taken priority over freedom and law over justice. . . . But if God is doing the first, then the concrete realities are those *not yet given* patterns and structures that are displacing patterns and structures that have been taken for granted; then freedom is the presupposition and condition of order, and justice is the foundation and criterion of law.[11]

The civil rights movement, though it may not have put the matter in such terms, operated on the conviction that God was indeed at work upholding the world by changing it, and what they were doing was, therefore, in significant measure a matter of being co-workers with God. This outlook was uniquely able to sustain all who were committed to the struggle through the anguished and difficult testings of those years.

This sense of possibility was also strengthened by a conviction, which blends emphases of both social gospel liberalism and Christian realism, that the yearning of people for the achievement of dignity represents a judgment of God upon any structures or practices in a society which deny such status to persons. While we cannot claim that every movement for liberation is an authentic bearer of the revolutionary intention of God, we can see in many movements of our day—and can see it clearly in the civil rights movement—a way by which God makes plain that a new order is needed and that structures which impede the inauguration of such an order are doomed to fall. This radical insight roots struggle not simply in human aspirations but in the God who impinges upon all events. Long in coming, the moment arrived when the system was revealed in all its iniquity, an offense not only to humanity but to God himself. He had judged it; he had condemned it; and the movement became the instrument in his hand for destroying the malignant power of oppression.

Care must be taken at this point. Nothing that has been said is intended to argue that the struggle is over or that a total victory has been won. No one can claim any such thing. Much remains to be done and the struggle is still to be carried on. While it is important in the interest of compassion to note what yet needs to be done, it is also important in the interest of accuracy to note that gains have been made. It is one thing to say that not everything has been done; all would agree with that. It is quite another thing to say that nothing has been done; that statement fails to take account of facts which can be seen by anybody. Remembering the emphasis given to the need for some sense of making an impact upon events, Christians in the eighties will be better prepared to continue the struggle if it can be realized that past struggles were not empty gestures.

One of the most impressive qualities in *My Soul Is Rested* is the testimony borne by participants to a real change. Raines himself affirms that the movement "transformed the South from a region of despair to the new heartland of American optimism."[12] He believes that Martin Luther King, Jr., if he had lived, would now see a South burdened with many remaining problems, but he would also "see a region changed in a way that millions of us who lacked his vision would have thought impossible twenty years ago. He would see a South where we are all free at last to become what we can."[13]

Howell Raines speaks as a white Southerner. Albert Turner, a black participant in the struggle, makes a similar affirmation: "There has really been a change here. Things ain't what we'd like to see, but let's face it. It ain't ten years ago. I'll be forty my birthday next and I don't need to ask nobody if there has been a change. . . . The mere fact that I'm the manager here is a big thing." [14] There are many other opinions of the same sort, but let one more suffice:

> "I was twenty-three when I joined SCLC and was about thirty-three, thirty-four when I left there," said J. T. Johnson. "Folks tell me sometimes about it was a waste of time . . . they don't realize the work that we've done, they are reapin' the results of it, and had we not done that, they never would have been where they are today . . . especially the younger generation, they don't realize what happened in the sixties . . . nobody talks about it. Nobody teaches them what happened . . . I should have gotten a job teachin' about the sixties . . . so the kids today would understand *how* and *why* . . . It's not because it came on a platter, but people worked hard, people even died. . . ." [15]

It is crucially important that this dimension of the struggle of the sixties be kept before us. It is one of the epic stories of our history, and in coming generations this gripping tale will be a source of pride which will take its rightful place with other great episodes in American history.

The Temptations of Violence

The possibility of significant action in human history was not the only way in which the civil rights movement of the sixties illustrated the principles we have set forth. The steadfast reliance upon love as the technique of nonviolent action provides validation of a fundamental principle.

As we have seen, Martin Luther King, Jr., had come to his position out of study and reflection. Thoreau, Gandhi, Rauschenbusch, and Niebuhr all contributed insights which he then fused into a way of action. It should be noted, however, that King was not an absolute pacifist, except perhaps for his early years. This position he, like many others, abandoned after exposure to Reinhold Niebuhr's thought. But he nevertheless saw with penetrating insight, perhaps prompted by Niebuhr's analysis in *Moral Man and Immoral Society*, that nonviolence was the only strategy which held out the possibility of success.

The commitment to nonviolent action can be seen as the utilization of a technique emphasized in Gandhi and social gospel liberalism, to which was added the insight from Niebuhr that social change does not come about without the application of pressure. For a long time blacks in the South and elsewhere had taken with incredible fortitude the injustices of the white society. Such forebearance, if not unnoticed, was surely ineffectual. Liberation from oppression and injustice would be forever delayed if blacks did nothing more. No change would ever be brought about unless dramatic and demanding actions were taken. The bus boycott, the sit-ins, the marches—these were actions which put considerable pressure on the white society. Not only did the nonviolent action put all kinds of pressure on the white community, but it had another advantage as well. Great sections of the white community, hitherto largely indifferent to the fate of blacks, were won over to sympathy and in many instances to active involvement. While violence was later to alienate these sectors of the population, it was the genius of Martin Luther King to enlist the moral support of this significant bloc of persons. They provided an atmosphere of support which should never be discounted.

The nonviolent action had a way of disarming even the most violent. One time, for example, the Ku Klux Klan scheduled a march into Montgomery. King and the leaders talked about what should be done, and said, "Ah! Tell everybody to put on their Sunday clothes, stand on their steps, and when the Ku Kluxers come, applaud 'em." [16] The Ku Kluxers came, marched three blocks, and left. They could do nothing in the face of a people whom they could not reduce to fear.

It was never easy, of course, to maintain the commitment to nonviolence. The Jim Clarks and the Bull Connors stretched to the limit the capacity of the movement to refrain from retaliatory violence. Only the enormous prestige and self-discipline of Martin Luther King kept the movement in his days firmly committed to nonviolence. It is hardly surprising that his removal by the assassin's bullet should have unleashed pent-up feelings that were expressed in the violence which came to characterize the movement itself. With King's charismatic presence removed, the way was opened for the Carmichaels and others who espoused a wholly different sort of strategy.

The strains of "We Shall Overcome," sung by whites and blacks together in the days of Selma and Montgomery, were drowned by the cries of "Burn, baby, burn." A movement which had united blacks and whites in a common cause was torn asunder by advocates of black power. The militant took over, and violence, bloodshed, and burnings took place all across the land. No matter how understandable from certain perspectives the violence may have been, it had the unfortunate result of tearing apart the solidarity of the civil rights movement and losing the goodwill of large sections of the population, black as well as white. What took place in that time—roughly the late sixties and early seventies—was a strange phenomenon in which intellectuals and ecclesiastics indulged in a romantic flirtation with violence itself. It was a sad performance.

We have not emerged from this period. It is, therefore, important to look at the issue of violence, since some today tend to justify it without any kind of careful analysis of its theological justification or its practical effectiveness. In both intellectuals and ecclesiastics there is a blindness to the whole issue of violence. Perhaps because their lives are spent in cloistered surroundings amid bloodless books and gentle souls, the two groups are not very well equipped to understand violence. One suspects that much of what is said by either group is a result of the fact that they tend to read the pronouncements about revolutionary intentions and to ignore the character of revolutionary or terrorist deeds. The intellectual is conditioned to approve if the statements as issued sound cogent and vaguely liberal. The ecclesiastic tends to approve if the statements as issued sound morally lofty. Neither group does much to probe behind the words, and neither looks at what is actually done.

Both of these groups tend to employ a rhetoric which is violent in statement in order to lend an aura of excitement to an intention that is not even mildly interesting. The academic who cries out, "To the barricades!"often means, "Let us approach the lectern with all deliberate speed." The fascination with violence for both groups is often in direct proportion to its distance from them.

Certain elements of modern outlook combine to produce this confusion about violence. Conor Cruise O'Brien, in an Oxford lecture on "Liberty and Terror," suggests three factors which operate today to justify violence. One is "the sense of guilt which many educated middle-class people feel about the privileges they possess, and which of course they don't want to give up." They then pride themselves on being detached from the democratic system and applaud the violent terrorist who in striking out is imagined to be striking out at these democratic shams. A second source is the assumption of neutrality, using professional detachment as a way by which to avoid any kind of judgment. O'Brien illustrates this in the case of a journalist who, in the Herrema kidnapping, prided himself on neither condemning nor condoning either side. "A certain number of journalists, academics, clergymen and others seem to have a somewhat similar concept of professional detachment." The third element is a sentimentalizing of the terrorist. At work, say some, is simply a case of misguided idealism, and this is honorable because the sentimentalist assumes that a willingness to run risks is a proof of moral superiority.[17]

To these should be added a couple of other elements which may help to explain the currently fashionable defense of violence. We suffer from a seriously misleading concept of human rights. The "imperial self," to use Quentin Anderson's term, has moved to the center. This self is to be granted, immediately and without question, whatever the self wants. The legitimate claims of a social order are hardly worth comparing with the regal needs of this individual, and if society gets in the way, then society can be rent asunder in order to satisfy the wants or rights of this person. Henry Fairlie writes:

> Any felt need or desire or longing, for anything which one lacks and someone else has, is today conceived to be a right which, when demanded, must be conceded without challenge; and if it is not at once conceded, the claimants are entitled to be angry. We can hardly blame the claimants for taking advantage of this foolishness, for they are justified in advance on four grounds: what they want, it is their right to have; when it is asked, it should be granted; if it is not granted, it is understandable that they get angry; and since they are angry, their demand must in the first place have been justified.[18]

Back of much of the violence of the sixties was this idea that society has no rights, only persons have them, and such rights are to be instantly gratified.

It would be unrealistic not to note also that violence has a powerful lure for human beings. This was hinted at in some of the comments made about intellectuals and ecclesiastics, who are perhaps the best examples since they might be expected to be least susceptible to the seduction of violence. The fact that they not only can tolerate violence but also condone it and develop a rationale by which to justify it is added confirmation of its powerful hold on human beings. "One of the reasons we have made so little progress in our mitigating of violence," writes Rollo May, "is that we have determinedly overlooked the elements in it that are attractive, alluring, and fascinating."[19] The start of any helpful dealing with violence is the realistic recognition of this psychological truth.

The upshot of all this is to suggest that Christian social action in the eighties needs to be extremely careful in its utilization of violence. This approach is not a doctrinaire, abstract repudiation of violence, nor is it based on an unawareness of the different kinds of violence which are practiced. An adequate Christian social theory for the eighties very much needs to recognize that overt violence, which destroys lives and property, is by no means the only type of violence. If we should be on guard against such acts of violence, we should be just as much on guard against that violence which does not kill but simply starves to death. The moral difference between the two types of violence is not very great.

To any contemplation of the use of violence we need to apply, as Richard John Neuhaus and Robert McAfee Brown suggest, the tests of the just war. Neuhaus says:

> A just war is a war: (1) that is declared by legitimate public authority; (2) that is in response to a real injury that has been suffered; (3) that is undertaken only after all reasonable means of peaceful settlement have been exhausted; (4) in which those prosecuting the war have good intention; (5) in which damage likely to be incurred by the war will not be disproportionate to the injury suffered; (6) that employs only legitimate and moral means; (7) in which there is reasonable hope for success.[20]

When these tests are applied to violence and revolution, they make the utilization of such violence extremely questionable. It is not ruled out absolutely, because there may well be some situations in which justice can be served by no other means. Robert McAfee Brown, after listing these same tests, arrives at a helpful conclusion: "What will have to be demonstrated with overwhelming certainty will not be that violence can be repudiated but that it can be employed. The use of violence will always remain the exception rather than the rule."[21]

The early days of the civil rights movement provided a heartening illustration of the power of nonviolence to effect significant changes in society. This demonstration must surely be part of the spiritual preparation we make for our life in the decade of the eighties.

An Invaluable Legacy

Christian social action in the eighties needs not only to renounce the lethargy of the seventies and to recover the zeal of the sixties but also to learn to channel the zeal with greater effectiveness. This can be done only if there is a careful evaluation of that period, which has been attempted here in centering attention on the civil rights struggle. These pages have tried to make clear the fact that we have immensely valuable resources. The past has left a helpful legacy in the insights and labors of great figures in social gospel liberalism and in Christian realism. Most of all, as this chapter has claimed, we have seen how such elements became fused in a life which, despite its brevity, left an abiding legacy. In Martin Luther King, Jr., and in the elements which he utilized creatively in working out the strategy in Montgomery, Selma, Washington, and elsewhere, we have a dynamic reminder that Christian faith has an abiding capacity both to produce ennobling visions and to inspire self-sacrificing deeds. Such a legacy may well prepare us, if we will reflect seriously on it, for whatever forms Christian social strategy may require in the eighties.

Chart for Rough Waters

This book has a simple thesis. Christian mission, no matter in what age it is carried on, requires involvement in social and political issues. The decade of the sixties, whatever its defects, deserves commendation for being so involved. In contrast, the seventies have been years in which, in terms of our figure of speech, the ecclesiastical ship has been in port. Perhaps this was a necessary respite; let that be granted. Now is the time, repairs having been made, some cargo having been removed and new cargo taken aboard, directions and destinations having been checked, to head for open seas.

Of course, there will be rough periods. The seas will be hazardous, and great demands will be made upon those who sail the craft. Some charts for rough water will be needed, and these final pages are an attempt to suggest some guidelines. The reflections are offered with the decade of the eighties particularly in mind.

Throughout these pages there has been a refrain. Serious disservice is done to Christian social action when we fail to see that we can afford neither bleak despair nor sunny confidence. Whenever we have permitted our hopes to lose linkage to the possible, we have suffered a failure of nerve. The same emotional experience overcomes those who are gripped by a sense of total hopelessness. How, then, can we look toward mission in the eighties without falling victim to either of these viewpoints? Our first guideline emerges to help: *our responsibility is to venture in faith; success is not our fundamental concern.*

It would be naive to imagine that this is an easy guideline by which to live. Particularly in America, the great thing is to be successful. This drive toward success has deeply infiltrated the outlook of Christians. As we have seen, triumphalism was a powerful current in social gospel thinking, and this outlook continues to flow, a bit submerged in the light of current disenchantment, but nevertheless very much present beneath the surface. If success does not justify effort, a culture which lacks vibrant theological resources has nothing else to put in its place. Accordingly, to suggest that Christians are called to venture and to leave the results of the venturing in the hands of God is to speak a language foreign to secular culture and, unfortunately, foreign to much of the culture of the churches. At this point we see the accuracy of Earl Brill's comment that what we have in this land is not so much a case of the churches making America religious as the secular society making religion American.[1] The centrality of the success drive is a cogent illustration of this very point.

The complexity of the matter emerges in the realization that if we cannot make success the criterion, neither are we allowed to find a kind of self-righteous vindication in failure. It is a narrow line which must be walked. The Christian in social action cannot indulge in the luxury of investing every effort with the noble aura of a lost cause. The sole criterion must be grateful response to the love of God. If such response results in observable improvements in the quality of our social order, rejoicing is surely proper. If, however, the efforts fail to produce impressive, visible gains, there is no excuse for despair. We have done what responsive love enjoins. We can neither be expected to do more nor permitted to do less.

A work of imaginative literature provides a parable for our venture. The contemporary mood is graphically portrayed in Ernest Hemingway's brief and beautiful book *The Old Man and the Sea.*[2] In so many ways, the story of Santiago is a fitting parable of our struggle with social evils. The old man, "thin and gaunt," had fished for eighty-four days with no luck at all. The next day he put out alone, and when he was far from shore, he set his lines with the precision of a craftsman. Suddenly, a hundred feet below the surface, a marlin took the bait. The old fisherman knew he had a great catch, perhaps the greatest of his career. It was an epic struggle; he felt the lines tear his hands to bloody pulp and lacerate his back when he wound the straining lines around himself. Finally, the great fish gave up. Santiago, affirming that "man is not made for defeat," lashed the fish to the side and headed for shore. But soon the sharks came, and in attack after attack they ripped the marlin of all flesh until only the bones remained. When Santiago reached shore, he had only bleeding hands, a torn back, and a gigantic skeleton. He knew what had happened: he had gone out "too far."

The parallels are clear. Confronting social evils, many moderns believed that they had achieved a victory never before won by human beings. It had not, of course, come without struggle; there were bleeding hands and torn backs. But the greatness of the catch made it seem, at least for a time, supremely worthwhile. It was not until they sought to embody the victory in definite structures that they discovered, like Santiago, that they really had only a skeleton. Then they, too, understood that they had gone out "too far."

That story, better than the essentially meaningless task of Sisyphus, catches the contemporary mood. Curiously, Hemingway, though not a Christian, seemed driven almost in spite of himself to use Christian motifs. Dealing with an elemental reality, he found that the artist can probe such depths only by utilizing the accents of the Christian story. The wounds of Santiago, with his bleeding hands and back, recall another's wounds and stripes. The mast reminds the reader of a cross. Santiago begins his testing at noon of the first day and ends at noon on the third day—a sequence recalling the passion of Christ. He carries the mast back to the shack, stumbling and weary. And he flings himself down on his cot with his arms outstretched and his palms up as in crucifixion. These parallels are pointed out not to claim Hemingway for Christianity but to say that this faith has provided motifs whereby, even if unconsciously, the artist and the activist can make some sense out of today's struggles.

The parable is one which needs to be taken seriously. The task now is that of sustaining involvement in social witness when the only trophy that will be brought to shore is a skeleton picked clean by sharks. Santiago knew only that he had to go out, set his lines with precision, and do his work. Christians in the eighties can rightfully expect to know only that the task must be undertaken to make and keep life human and that such effort is our "reasonable service."

A second guideline is that *the maintenance of purity is not our goal.* The goal is the service of God and neighbor with the willingness to undergo some of the hazards which are bound to be part of any venture of social involvement. This is something which needs to be faced directly. Nobody will come away from social involvement with clean hands.

Usually, the attempt is made to counteract this by the assertion that politics is noble or that participation in politics involves no more moral and ethical compromises than any other field of human endeavor. Such a contention is probably true, but it is beside the point. The point is to acknowledge that politics does involve dirty hands but to keep that admission within the context of our Christian commitment. When this is done, there is a chance to see that purity is no more God's requirement than is success.

The quest for purity has been a strong force, however, in keeping Christians from a willingness to be involved in political and social issues. Refusing to face the fact that to act in any realm of human existence is to run the risk of dirty hands, Christians have imagined that hands are kept clean by staying out of such issues. What results, however, is not that hands are really clean; such inaction is a strong support for systems of iniquitous oppression. The refusal to be involved in direct action either of support or of opposition does not get the Christian out of responsibility; it simply means that by default the weight of the Christian is on the side of the status quo. To look frankly at the fact that moral and ethical neutrality is an impossibility is to recognize that we are involved in one way or another and our only choice is whether to be actively involved in seeking to aid the achievement of an order which seeks the liberation of the oppressed or to acquiesce in the continuation of present orders and structures.

The contemporary social order is one in which no neat and pure choices are confronted; this is a characteristic not only of this social order but also of any society which has ever existed. In the midst of such an order, however, what is required is the recognition that our choice is by no means whether to have clean or dirty hands; it is only whether we have dirty hands produced by a struggle to bring into being a society which provides opportunities for maximum human development of every person in the widest possible fellowship. Unless such a society is our constant aim, we may find our social order torn apart. Charles Péguy has a wise word: "People who insist on keeping their hands clean are likely to find themselves without hands."[3]

It should be stressed that recognition that dirty hands will inevitably accompany social action is not a blank check for Christians to use indiscriminately any methods they wish. As we stated in the discussion of the utilization of violence, Christians must continually keep all methods under rigorous ethical scrutiny. While this caution must not be permitted to lead to passivity, it should assure that all methods employed have been determined upon in light of a conviction that they will lead to ends appropriate for Christian action.

The concern with purity not only is apparent in the reluctance of Christians to be involved in social issues, but also it finds reflection in some who are involved but who look askance upon possible allies because such allies may not be "pure" in their ideological commitment. This was an outlook which broke apart hopeful coalitions in the sixties. Nobody could be accepted as an ally, it seemed, unless there was agreement on all details. The result was that groups became so pure they had no effective base; they could only congratulate themselves on their admirable consistency and find in that a substitute for any genuine effectiveness.

This proclivity finds expression in the frequent denunciations of the middle class. Ignoring the fact that this is a large and potentially influential element, the purists dismiss it with ill-concealed contempt. Yet it is clear that no movement for genuine social change has much chance of success in modern America which does not utilize the resources of the middle class. Diana Trilling has called for a Tocqueville to help us to understand our present ambivalence toward the very idea of the middle class, "that bulwark of American society which provides the economic sustenance of our idealism at the same time as, all anomalously, it nourishes the most lethal assaults on our tranquility."[4] She points out also that while the middle class embodies most of the assumptions and attitudes at which many are angry, it is nevertheless into the middle class that we seek to move those not now part of it.

To ignore a potential ally is not only a failure in strategy, but it is also a failure in the Christian community in terms of love and acceptance. It will be a major failure of the Christian churches if there is no capacity within the life of the fellowship to treat with respect those who differ. Such failure would be especially glaring if a capacity to respect while differing should be characteristic of the secular order. Willie Morris, in a discussion of the difference between his involvements in Mississippi and in Texas, affirmed that it was in Texas that he reached maturity. He writes:

> There it was politics, the ambivalent and exposed world of the politician, that taught me about the complexity of human affairs, about the irrelevance of most dogmatic formulas, about loyalty and courage and devotion to human causes. . . . One's faith and trust came to reside in the integrity and responsibility of a group of people, people with shared assumptions about reform and liberality, rather than in the superiority of certain groupings of ideas about society. . . . The best fighters for justice and humanity in Texas were the best human beings, dealing compassionately with the enemy even in the heat of the fight.[5]

If such behavior is possible in the secular political order, surely nothing less should mark the Christian community.

To these two guidelines for social action in the eighties—fidelity rather than success as the determining characteristic and love of neighbor rather than abstract purity as the inspiration of action— should be added *a determination not to be tyrannized by the demand to be specific.* Christian social action has sometimes been hampered in the past by a demand that all the specifics must be worked out by Christian forces if they expect to have any right to speak. Unless all the specifics are spelled out, it is expected that Christian churches will refrain from expressing any judgment.

There was a time when this position seemed to be quite persuasive. Unless the specifics, some of them technical in nature, were spelled out with precision, any Christian pronouncement could be dismissed as "idealistic" or "utopian" or "irresponsible." While some of the dismissal was done out of sincere spirit, much of it was a technique admirably suited to maintain things as they are. No change could be thought about unless and until every technical detail was adequately provided for. Even within Christian churches there was a disposition to agree to this sort of proposal.

If, however, the independence of the churches is to be maintained, a refusal to get bogged down in the specifics becomes an effective strategy. This does not mean a cavalier dismissal of concern for technical matters; it simply asserts that the distinctive contribution of the churches is to be found in setting forth the goals for human existence which arise out of faith and in keeping enough distance from the specifics to be able to judge all policies from an independent stance. In so doing, the churches will be filling a role which no other institution is so ideally suited to undertake.

As another has well said, it is the task of the churches to proclaim,

> "But let justice roll down like waters,
>   and righteousness like an everflowing stream."
> —Amos 5:24

The problems of irrigation and so forth can be left to the technicians!

A final guideline will perhaps sound strange in light of the fundamental thesis of this book. *Social action and political involvement, while important, are only part of faith.* Such action is one aspect of our response as Christian people to what God has done and what he calls us to join him in doing now. All that has been said in these pages has sought to make clear that this response is basic and inescapable. At the same time, it is necessary to sound a warning against those who would make this aspect of faith the only or even the decisive evidence of Christian commitment. It is important: it is not the exclusive mark of our Christian calling.

Strangely enough, there is every chance that Christians will be more effective in social action if this subtle but important distinction is kept in mind. We have tended in this day and age to invest political action with a redemptive significance. Our willingness to be so involved has tended to become the way by which we achieve our redemption. There is a danger that we will relapse into works righteousness once again, this time trusting not in "religious" but in political works to assure us of redemption. Hence we tend to grow frenzied in our efforts, often sacrificing in the process our discernment and even more often losing our compassion. Our social action would be relieved of its quality of frenzy if we could bear in mind that the motivation for such action is not to achieve redemption but simply to bear witness to a redemption already given us by God. We join in works of social witness, not in order to be redeemed, but because we have been redeemed.

Moreover, our social action becomes frenzied and often ineffective because we believe the new order must be realized here on earth within the bounds of our history. Since the dimension of the eternal has so faded from Christian existence, we feel that everything must be done—and done now. There is no sense—or there is too little sense—of the kingdom as an order which in its deepest dimension is both a present reality and a future consummation, to be brought about in God's own time. To take seriously the realization that in history there is not and never will be such a thing as perfection is to be prepared to live in the midst of many imperfections and not to be devastated by such a situation. The Christian, always a stranger and a pilgrim, can rest finally, as Augustine knew, only in God. No order of things, however good it may be, can ever be the Christian's real dwelling. The heart is restless until it rests in God.

It is for this reason that the Christian should always be able to have a somewhat detached attitude toward political action. We share in it, because it is a way by which we respond to God's love; but we do not expect too much of it. Carl Becker in one of his essays put well the position which knows political action to be important but denies that it is redemptive. He writes:

> The real Leviathan is not government, but society—this amazing and vital and arresting and formidable phenomenon we call American civilization. What can we do with it? Very little since we too are a part of it. . . . We can at best play our part, perform our function, cultivate our gardens. Some there will always be whose gardens are in the vicinity of Capitol Hill. Well, it's an indifferent soil, but there's plenty of manure. Something may grow even there.[6]

A final word must be added. Everything for which these pages have pleaded rests upon the recovery by the churches of a vital theological outlook. No life of social action, in the eighties or at any other time, can be sustained over the long run apart from rootage in a vibrant Christian faith. The ship will be ready for open seas only if there is a renewed sense on the part of the churches of what it means to live a life of faith in these days. No timid, hesitant equivocation will do.

Strong convictions about God's grace and the way he moves within our history will alone enable Christians to face the challenges of the eighties. Perhaps what we need is in the words of a woman of the Gaelic race who said, "I know the secret of happy living. 'Tis ever to sail the seas and ever to keep the heart in port."[7]

Notes

Prologue: Two Cheers for the Sixties

[1] This Prologue is based on my article, "Viewpoints: Two Cheers for the Sixties," *Foundations,* October-December, 1976, pp. 292-297.

[2] Robert Penn Warren, *Democracy and Poetry* (Cambridge: Harvard University Press, 1975), p. 87.

[3] Alexander M. Bickel, *The Morality of Consent* (New Haven: Yale University Press, 1975), p. 113.

[4] John C. Bennett, "Silence on Issues of High Priority," *Worldview*, May, 1975, pp. 23-24.

[5] Martin E. Marty, *The Fire We Can Light* (Garden City: Doubleday & Co., Inc., 1973), pp. 19-20.

Chapter 1   Our Present Plight

[1] Robert Coles, *Farewell to the South* (Boston: Little, Brown & Company, 1972), pp. 238-239.

[2] Quoted by D. R. Sharpe, *Walter Rauschenbusch* (New York: The Macmillan Co., 1942), p. 222.

[3] Walter Rauschenbusch, *A Theology for the Social Gospel* (Nashville: Abingdon Press, 1945), pp. 142-143. Copyright 1917 by Macmillan Publishing Co., Inc., renewed 1945 by Pauline Rauschenbusch.

[4] *The Kingdom,* vol. 1, no. 2 (September, 1907); quoted in Sharpe, *op. cit.*, p. 138.

[5] Reinhold Niebuhr, *Moral Man and Immoral Society* (New York: Charles Scribner's Sons, 1932), pp. 21-22.

[6] Godfrey Hodgson, *America in Our Time* (Garden City: Doubleday & Co., Inc., 1976), p. 198.

[7] *Ibid.*, p. 199.

[8] George H. Sabine, "Carl Lotus Becker," in Carl Becker, *Freedom and Responsibility in the American Way of Life* (New York: Alfred A. Knopf, Inc., 1945; Vintage Books, Inc., 1955), p. xlviii.

Chapter 2   The Need for Independence

[1] H. Richard Niebuhr, Wilhelm Pauck, Francis P. Miller, *The Church Against the World* (Chicago: Willett, Clark & Co., 1935), p. 1.

[2] *Ibid.*, p. 3.

[3] *Ibid.*, p. 4.

[4] *Ibid.*, p. 11.

[5] *Ibid.*, p. 102.

[6] See Albert van den Heuvel, *These Rebellious Powers* (London: SCM Press, 1966).

[7] Arthur M. Schlesinger, Sr., *Paths to the Present* (Boston: Houghton Mifflin Company, 1964), pp. 89-103; the essay first appeared in *The Yale Review* in 1939.

[8] See my essay "The Tides of Christian Social Action," *Religion in Life*, Winter, 1974, pp. 482-493; some paragraphs from the essay are used on pages 40 to 43. Used by permission of *Religion in Life* and Abingdon Press.

[9] Frederick Lewis Allen, *Only Yesterday* (New York: Harper & Row, Publishers, 1931), p. 13.

[10] *Ibid.*, p. 21.

[11] Robert T. Handy, *A Christian America: Protestant Hopes and Historical Realities* (New York: Oxford University Press, 1971), p. 189.

[12] *Ibid.*, p. 200.

[13] Martin Marty, *The New Shape of American Religion* (New York: Harper & Row, Publishers, 1959), p. 79.

[14] William Lee Miller, *Piety Along the Potomac* (Boston: Houghton Mifflin Company, 1964), p. 129.

[15] John R. Earle, Dean D. Knudsen, Donald W. Shriver, Jr., *Spindles and Spires* (Atlanta: John Knox Press, 1976), pp. 201-202. Copyright © 1976 John Knox Press. Used by permission.

[16] Quoted in Cushing Strout, *The New Heavens and the New Earth* (New York: Harper & Row, Publishers, 1974), p. 250.

[17] C. Wright Mills, *The Causes of World War Three* (New York: Simon & Schuster, Inc., 1958), p. 148.

[18] John C. Bennett, *Christianity—and our World* (New York: Association Press, 1936), p. 1.

[19] Dietrich Bonhoeffer, *Letters and Papers from Prison,* ed. Eberhard Bethge (New York: The Macmillan Co., 1953), pp. 194-195.

[20] Jacques Ellul, *A Critique of the New Commonplaces* (New York: Alfred A. Knopf, Inc., 1968), pp. 75-76.

[21] P. T. Forsyth, *Positive Preaching and the Modern Mind* (Grand Rapids: Wm. B. Eerdmans Publishing Co., First American Edition, 1964), p. 79.

Chapter 3   Churches and the Passing of Christendom

[1] See William R. Hutchison, *The Modernist Impulse in American Protestantism* (Cambridge: Harvard University Press, 1976), pp. 302-303.

[2] Robert T. Handy, *A Christian America: Protestant Hopes and Historical Realities* (New York: Oxford University Press, 1971), p. 12.

[3] See H. Richard Niebuhr, *Christ and Culture* (New York: Harper & Row, Publishers, 1951).

[4] Walter Rauschenbusch, *A Theology for the Social Gospel* (Nashville: Abingdon Press, 1945), p. 225.

[5] *Ibid.*, p. 226.

[6] Reinhold Niebuhr, *Christianity and Power Politics* (New York: Charles Scribner's Sons, 1946), p. 194.

[7] *Ibid.*, pp. 194-195.

[8] Quoted in Robert T. Handy, "The Long Spell of Christendom," *Soundings*, vol. 60, no. 2 (Summer, 1977), p. 129.

[9] Winthrop S. Hudson, "Denominationalism as a Basis for Ecumenicity," in Russell Richey, ed., *Denominationalism* (Nashville: Abingdon Press, 1977), p. 22.

[10] See Winthrop S. Hudson, *American Protestantism* (Chicago: The University of Chicago Press, 1961), pp. 40-44.

[11] Ernst Troeltsch, *The Social Teaching of the Christian Churches* (London: George Allen & Unwin Ltd., 1931), vol. I, p. 331.

[12] Lewis S. Mudge, "Searching for Faith's Social Reality," *The Christian Century*, September 22, 1976, p. 787. Copyright 1976 Christian Century Foundation. Reprinted by permission.

[13] Garry Wills, "Feminists and Other Useful Fanatics," *Harper's Magazine*, June, 1976, p. 35. Copyright© 1976 by *Harper's Magazine*. All rights reserved. Reprinted by special permission.

[14] *Ibid.*

[15] *Ibid.*, p. 38.

[16] *Ibid.*, p. 40.

[17] *Ibid.*, p. 42.

Chapter 4   The Power of Weakness and the Weakness of Power

[1] Bertrand Russell, *Power: A New Social Analysis* (New York: W. W. Norton &Co., Inc., 1938).

[2] Paul Lehmann, *The Transfiguration of Politics* (New York: Harper & Row, Publishers, 1975), p. 27.

[3] Robert T. Handy, *A Christian America: Protestant Hopes and Historical Realities* (New York: Oxford University Press, 1971), Chapter VII.

[4] Jürgen Moltmann, *The Crucified God* (New York: Harper & Row, Publishers, 1973), pp. 249-250.

[5] Geddes MacGregor, *He Who Lets Us Be* (New York: The Seabury Press, Inc., 1975), p. 167.

[6] *Ibid.*, p. 168.

[7] *Ibid.*, p. 143.

[8] John Oman, *Grace and Personality* (New York: Macmillan, Inc., 1925), p. 14.

[9] "The Talk of the Town," *The New Yorker*, February 21, 1977, p. 27. From Notes and Comments in *The New Yorker*, reprinted by permission; © 1977 The New Yorker Magazine, Inc.

[10] Adolf A. Berle, *Power* (New York: Harcourt Brace Jovanovich, Inc., 1969), pp. 126-127.

[11] Quoted by John Corry, "God, Country, and Billy Graham," *Harper's Magazine*, February 1969, p. 37.

[12] Quoted by Harvey Bates, "Letters from Ernest," *The Christian Century*, March 9, 1977, p. 219.

[13] Karl Barth, *Church Dogmatics* (Edinburgh: T. & T. Clark, 1957), vol. 2, Part I, p. 386.

[14] Lehmann, *op. cit.*, p. 122.

[15] *Ibid.*, p. xiii.

[16] H. Richard Niebuhr, "War as the Judgment of God," *The Christian Century*, May 13, 1942, p. 630.

[17] *Ibid.*, p. 632.

[18] H. Richard Niebuhr, "War as Crucifixion," *The Christian Century*, April 28, 1943, p. 515.

Chapter 5   The Radical Middle

[1] George Steiner, "True to Life," *The New Yorker*, March 29, 1969, p. 143.

[2] George Santayana, *Winds of Doctrine;* quoted in Henry Steele Commager, *The American Mind* (New Haven: Yale University Press, 1950), p. 120.

[3] Harvey Cox, "Christian Realism: Retrospect and Prospect," *Christianity and Crisis,* August 5, 1968, p. 181. Copyright © 1968 by Christianity and Crisis, Inc.

[4] Reinhold Niebuhr, *The Nature and Destiny of Man*, vol. 1 (New York: Charles Scribner's Sons, 1947), p. 183.

[5] Reinhold Niebuhr, *Christianity and Power Politics* (New York: Charles Scribner's Sons, 1946), pp. 75-76.

[6] Robert E. Fitch, "Reinhold Niebuhr's Philosophy of History," in Charles W. Kegley and Robert W. Bretall, *Reinhold Niebuhr: His Religious, Social and Political Thought* (New York: The Macmillan Co., 1956), pp. 293-294.

[7] Reinhold Niebuhr, *Christianity and Power Politics,* p. 200.

[8] Alexander Miller, *The Renewal of Man* (London: Victor Gollanz Ltd., 1956), p. 38.

[9] Nat Hentoff, "Dehumanized Radicalism," *Mademoiselle*, May 1969, p. 16; quoted in Lloyd J. Averill, *The Problem of Being Human* (Valley Forge: Judson Press, 1974), p. 68.

Chapter 6   Tried in a Crucible

[1] Martin Luther King, Jr., *Stride Toward Freedom* (New York: Harper & Row, Publishers, Perennial Library, 1958), p. 72.

[2] *Ibid.*, p. 73.

[3] *Ibid.*

[4] Kenneth L. Smith and Ira G. Zepp, Jr., *Search for the Beloved Community: The Thinking of Martin Luther King, Jr.* (Valley Forge: Judson Press, 1974), p. 71.

[5] Reinhold Niebuhr, *Moral Man and Immoral Society* (New York: Charles Scribner's Sons, 1932), p. 254.

[6] Quoted in Smith and Zepp, *op. cit.*, p. 97; the quotation is from *Love and Justice: Selections from the Shorter Writings of Reinhold Niebuhr*, edited by D. B. Robertson (New York: The World Publishing Co., Meridian Books, 1967), p. 20.

[7] *Ibid.*, p. 97.

[8] Howell Raines, *My Soul Is Rested* (New York: G. P. Putnam's Sons, 1977), p. 17.

[9] *Ibid.*

[10] *Ibid.*, p. 23.

[11] Paul Lehmann, *The Transfiguration of Politics* (New York: Harper & Row, Publishers, 1975), p. 263.

[12] Raines, *op. cit.*, p. 20.

[13] *Ibid.*, pp. 23-24.

[14] *Ibid.*, p. 187.

[15] *Ibid.*, p. 456.

[16] *Ibid.*, p. 56.

[17] Conor Cruise O'Brien, "Liberty and Terror: Illusions of Violence, Delusions of Liberation," *Encounter*, October, 1977, p. 40.

[18] Henry Fairlie, "Anger or Ira," *The New Republic*, September 24, 1977, p. 19.

[19] Rollo May, *Power and Innocence* (New York: W. W. Norton & Co., Inc., 1972), p. 165.

[20] Peter L. Berger and Richard John Neuhaus, *Movement and Revolution* (Garden City: Doubleday & Company, Inc., Anchor Book, 1970), p. 163.

[21] Robert McAfee Brown, *Religion and Violence* (Philadelphia: The Westminster Press, 1973), p. 87.

Epilogue: Chart for Rough Waters

[1] Earl H. Brill, *The Future of the American Past* (New York: The Seabury Press, Inc., 1974), pp. 12-13.

[2] These paragraphs (from pp. 112-114) are taken from my article "The Bosford Declaration," *The Christian Century*, August 18-25, 1976, p. 707. Copyright © 1976 Christian Century Foundation. Reprinted by permission.

[3] Quoted in William Sloane Coffin, Jr., *Once to Every Man* (New York: Atheneum Publishers, 1977), pp. 32-33.

[4] Diana Trilling, *We Must March My Darlings* (New York: Harcourt Brace Jovanovich, 1977), p. 280.

[5] Willie Morris, *North Toward Home* (Boston: Houghton Mifflin Co., 1967), p. 309.

[6] Carl L. Becker, *Everyman His Own Historian* (New York: F. S. Crofts & Co., 1935), pp. 89-90.

[7] Alistair MacLean, *High Country* (New York: Charles Scribner's Sons, 1952), p. 8.